CYBERCRIME:

How to Stay Safe from Online Fraud and Identity Theft

By Retired FBI Special Agent

Jeff Lanza

Communications Dynamics Publishing
Mission, Kansas
Copyright © 2019, 2017
by Jeff Lanza

All rights reserved.
Published in the United States by
Communication Dynamics, LLC.

ISBN 978-0-692-93474-6

Printed in United States of America
Cover design by Melanie Rutherford
Second Edition

The opinions expressed in this book are entirely those of Jeff Lanza and not those of the FBI.

To Pam, my wife, and our two children, Christopher and Angela and to my father, Anthony and my brother, Tommy, who both passed away in 2016.

Contents

Introduction
Part 1 - Preventing Identity Theft and Other Frauds
Chapter 1   Credit Card Fraud 1

Chapter 2   Identity Theft 5

Chapter 3   Emotions 27

Part Two - Preventing Cybercrime

Chapter 4   Malware 37

Chapter 5   Phishing 45

Chapter 6   Ransomware 57

Chapter 7   Bank Account Takeovers 65

Chapter 8   Email Account Hijacking 77

Chapter 9   Passwords 89

Chapter 10   Two-Factor Authentication 101

Chapter 11   Wi-Fi Security 109

Chapter 12   Antivirus Software 117

Chapter 13   Mobile Security 125

               Summary 133

               Appendix A 135

               Appendix B 137

               Appendix C 139

               Acknowledgements 141

               About the Author 144

Introduction

The FBI, formerly known as the Bureau of Investigation, has been in existence since 1908. The agency was renamed the Federal Bureau of Investigation in 1935. In its early days, the FBI fought a major crime epidemic of the time, involving criminals commonly referred to as hoodlums. The hoodlums consisted of characters such as Machine Gun Kelly, Pretty Boy Floyd, and Baby Face Nelson.

In the 1970s, the FBI fought a crime epidemic involving mobsters, commonly referred to as the Mafia. Targets of federal investigations included people named Carlo Gambino, Sam Giancana, and Paul Castellano.

Today, the FBI is fighting a crime epidemic involving hackers. What's different about today's crime epidemic is that we all have to be part of the solution. In the 1930s and in the 1970s, the fight was mainly between law enforcement and criminals. But today's crime epidemic cannot be defeated by law enforcement alone. A main impediment that law enforcement faces today is that much of the criminal computer hacking that we see originates outside of U.S. borders. In some cases, the FBI is allowed to work with other countries and investigate fraud that originates in those places. But in most situations, the FBI is not allowed access to the top-tier criminals. Why would they be allowed this access when some of the top hackers around the world are bringing copious amounts of money stolen from U.S. businesses and individuals into their countries' economies?

For example, one hacker, Evgeniy Bogachev, is believed to be in Russia. According to the FBI and his wanted poster, as of March 2019, he has stolen over one hundred million dollars from U.S. businesses. He is considered such a threat that, as of this writing, he is one of the FBI's most wanted cyber criminals. Yet Russia has made no attempt to apprehend him, and even if they did, the U.S. has no way to extradite him, as there is no formal agreement between the two countries. The United States faces the same obstacle when it comes to other countries where known hackers live and work, such as Ukraine and China.

For this reason, law enforcement needs your help. Everyone must be more careful online and take steps to protect personal information and money. It doesn't seem like it will be possible for law enforcement or the criminal justice system in the United States to arrest and bring to justice the crooks that are collectively responsible for stealing billions of dollars from the United States.

Therefore, some of the focus and responsibility must be taken up by the victims and potential victims. That's everyone reading this, whether you live in the United States or not. You are a target for fraud. The only way we can put the hackers behind today's crime epidemic out of business is to dry up their source of funds, and that source is all of us, individuals and businesses. We can do that, for the most part, by being careful and vigilant online.

This book is about how to stay safe from hackers. It's about how to protect yourself online from a plethora of scams that are designed to trick you into providing information, money, or both to crooks.

You will learn how to spot common tricks, like phishing emails and internet links that, if clicked on, may install viruses on your computer. We will get into the topic of computer passwords and password management. You will learn about antivirus software, Wi-Fi security and how to protect yourself from the epidemic of ransomware, wherein computer files are held for ransom.

Before we get into any of that, it is important that we discuss another very important topic: identity theft. This is a serious crime that can cause numerous long-term problems for victims. As with computer crime, identity theft is a crime that is best dealt with before it happens, rather than after, as the effects of victimization can last for weeks, months, or, in some cases, years. First, we will discuss credit card fraud, which is different than identity theft. It is important to understand how the two crimes differ before we talk about identity theft.

I worked as an FBI agent for over 20 years. In most cases, when the FBI investigated a crime involving identity theft or cyber fraud, the crime had already been committed. It was too late to prevent it from happening. When I retired from the Bureau a few years ago, my passion became helping to prevent these crimes. When I speak professionally about these topics, the goal of my presentations is prevention. That is also the goal of this book. I want to help ensure that these crimes don't happen to you.

In discussing the twin problems of identity theft and cyber fraud, I have endeavored to make the material as straightforward, non-technical and to-the-point as possible. If you want more detailed information, this book contains reference material in appendixes that will point you to more detailed sources. All right, are you ready to go? Then hang on to your hats and read on!

Chapter 1
Credit Card Fraud

A person told me that their credit card had been stolen. I asked if they had reported the theft to the police or credit card company. They said they had not. I asked them why they didn't report the theft. The person told me that they did not report the theft of the credit card because whoever stole it was spending less than their spouse.

There are very few of us these days who have not been directly impacted by some type of fraud. Recently, I was the victim of credit card fraud—and I learned about it while I was six miles above the earth.

I was traveling on an airplane that had Wi-Fi capability, so I had access to my email account while flying. Have you ever had Wi-Fi access in an airplane? If you have, then you're familiar with the "lightning-fast" speeds the airplane Wi-Fi offers, typically measured in download speeds of megabytes per century.

I was in the process of reviewing my emails on the airplane, at a painfully slow rate, when I saw an email whose subject line stood out above the others: "FRAUD ALERT!"

Click…nothing…click…nothing…nothing…blank page. Now at least I was making some progress. A few minutes later, the contents of the email came up on my screen and I learned that someone was trying to use my credit card in the state of New Jersey.

So, here was the situation: I was 33,000 feet above the state of New Mexico. Someone was trying to use my credit card in three different retail establishments in New Jersey. The problem with that scenario was that the credit card that they were trying to use was in my pocket. So how were these transactions possible?

They were possible because the crooks didn't have my physical card. They had made a duplicate of my card, which is also known as "cloning" a credit card. How did they get the information to clone my card? I don't know, and the truth is, sometimes you never know how crooks get your information to commit credit card fraud or other crimes like identity theft.

The important part of the story is that the charges were declined. This was a simple case of credit card fraud, with no real, long-term consequences for me. The credit card company recognized that the attempted charges may have been fraudulent, so they declined them all. But even if the charges had gone through, I would not have been liable for the money; the credit card company would have eaten that cost. I simply received a new credit card with a new sixteen- digit number and security code in the mail two days later. Besides changing some monthly auto payments that were automatically charged to the original credit card, nothing else really needed to be done.

Now, to be clear, we all pay the cost of fraud collectively, as its expense gets passed on to us as consumers. But in this case, no money was taken out of my pocket. It was just a small hassle that left me idly wondering how the crooks got my credit card number to begin with. I didn't worry about it for long, though, because this was a minor case of fraud, as compared to identity theft.

Credit card fraud is often confused with identity theft, but these are two very different things and it is very important to understand the distinction. Identify theft is discussed in the next chapter.

Here are some tips to prevent credit card fraud:

1. Make a copy or write down all the information on the front and back of all the credit cards you carry. If your purse or wallet is lost or stolen, you will know what is at risk and can contact the credit card companies to stop all charges.
2. Set alerts with your credit card company that notifies you by text message if there is a charge to your card over a threshold amount. You determine the threshold.
3. Review your credit card statements carefully and report any fraud as soon as possible.

Fake Notifications

It is also possible that an email containing the term "Fraud Alert", or something similar, could be a fake. Always be skeptical of these emails, as the fake ones are designed to send you to a page where you enter your login credentials and in doing so, provide them to the crooks that sent you the fake email. It is fine to look at the email, but you shouldn't provide any login information. In my case the email I received on the plane was really from my credit card company. It was not asking me to login, it was only notifying me of the attempted purchases.

Chapter 2
Identity Theft

"I don't need to worry about identity theft because no one wants to be me."

Jay London

Identity theft is very different from credit card fraud and much more serious. In identity theft cases, criminals obtain personally identifiable information such as your social security number, your birthdate, and your address. Of these, by far the most important for criminals is your social security number. That information is the most difficult to obtain and is the key to stealing your identity. What happens when they have your information?

Here are some things that criminals can do using your identity:

Open credit card accounts

Identity thieves sign up for credit cards in your name. The cards are sent to a different address and you have no knowledge that this has happened. They use the cards until they hit the credit limit. Eventually, the past due debt shows up on your credit report.

Open checking accounts

It's easy to open a checking account and order checks with a small amount of money online. The crook will overdraw the account, and in a worst-case scenario, a warrant is issued for your arrest for writing bad checks. This has happened to people I know.

Get loans

The crook uses your information to apply for a loan. Some examples are: car loans, home equity loans, and personal loans. Of course, they have no intention of paying the loan back to the lending institution.

If you learn that any financial accounts have been opened using your identity, you must contact the organization and advise them that the accounts were opened fraudulently.

You may require a police report and other indemnifying documentation to cancel the accounts.

File tax returns

Filing fraudulent tax returns has become a favorite crime of identity thieves. The criminals fill out a tax return using your identity. This crime occurs during tax filing season, which begins in January and ends in mid-April. The crook files early in the season, to beat you to it. The Internal Revenue Service accepts the crook's filing as your own and sends them an overpayment refund. The information the crook uses to file is made up, but it doesn't matter, as the IRS doesn't compare the information to any other documents until later. When you file your tax return, the IRS rejects it because you have already filed, according to them.

If this has happened to you, report it immediately to the IRS at this number: 1-800-908-4490. They will provide further instructions. You will likely get a PIN (personal identification number) to file your taxes in the future.

Get medical care

Medical identity theft occurs when someone uses your identity or insurance information to get medical treatment, prescription drugs, or surgery. This is a big concern for the entire health care industry, not only from a financial perspective, but because the crime may create false medical records for the identity theft victim.

Always check your health care statements carefully and report any inaccuracies to the health care provider and the health insurance agency.

File for social security benefits

If you are 62 years-of-age or older, you may be eligible to collect social security benefits. If a criminal has your social security number and other identifying information, they could create an online account at www.ssa.gov and direct your social security benefits to them.

If this happens, contact the Social Security Administration at this number: 1-800-269-0271 and follow their instructions. One way to prevent this from happening is to create an online account at www.ssa.gov. If you have an account created, a criminal can't create one and steal you benefits.

These are the most common examples of how your identity can be used for fraud. When these things happen, it is not as simple as taking a charge off a bill, as in the case of credit card fraud. The effects of identity theft can last a very long time and create a gigantic hassle in your life. This is the reason why identity theft prevention is so important. Generally, there are two sources of personal information for crooks: you, and any organization that holds your personal information. There are lots of things you can do or not do to protect personal information under your control, and we will talk about those methods first.

Here are some common ways crooks may get information that is under your control and how to help prevent it:

Method: They steal your mail.

Prevention: Use a locked mailbox where possible and register to receive online delivery of all financial correspondence. (We will talk about online security later in this book.) Also, don't put outgoing mail that contains sensitive information in your mailbox to be picked up. Take it to the post office.

Method: They take your trash.

Prevention: Use a secure shredder to shred documents containing personal information that's more than your name and address. (See the information box at the end of this chapter for what to shred and how to shred it.)

Method: They steal your wallet or purse.

Prevention: Don't carry your social security card or any document with your social security number in your wallet or purse.

Method: Fraudsters call you on the phone and trick you into providing information.

Prevention: Never provide personal information to anyone who calls you first! This is very important, so no matter what they say, if they have made an unsolicited call to you, seal your lips when it comes to personal information. Also, utilize caller ID to screen incoming calls. Let all calls from unrecognized numbers go to an answering machine and then decide later who should be called back.

Method: Your computer gets infected with malware, which allows crooks to steal information stored on your computer.

Prevention: Keep your computer protected with antivirus software and don't store documents containing social security numbers on your computer.

Method: You click on an internet link, sent to you by fraudsters that directs you to a website that asks for your social security number.

Prevention: Watch where you click! Don't click on links or attachments in emails from unknown senders. (The topic of computer crime will be discussed in much more detail later in this book.) Furthermore, never provide your social security number online unless it is for a reason described in this chapter.

Now let's discuss some common ways crooks may get information that is <u>not</u> under your control and what you can do when it happens:

Computer breaches. This could result from a couple of different scenarios: either an employee of an organization that has your personal information clicks on a phishing email that installs malware on an organization's computer network, or there is a direct hack into its computers. (This is what happened at Equifax, which you will read more about later in this chapter.)

Tricks. They use trickery to obtain your information from an employee. An example of this scenario is a fake email that looks like it is coming from the company CEO that asks for personal information.

Insiders. They use an employee who provides them with your information.

Theft. They steal an organization's trash that has not been properly shredded.

Many organizations house our personal information including schools, financial institutions, government agencies, and insurance companies, to name just a few. It is not our responsibility as customers or stakeholders of those organizations to protect the personal information that they store. We rely on others to do this. But in many cases, those responsible have not done a respectable job.

What we can do, however, is take preventative measures, or, in the case of a breach, reactive measures, which will be discussed shortly.

Protecting Your Social Security Number

Protecting your social security number (SSN) is one of the most important things you can do to prevent identity theft. Crooks can't open credit card accounts and bank accounts or file tax returns in your name without your SSN. For this reason, you must be careful about providing it to anyone.

Here are some legitimate reasons to provide your SSN to another person:

- You're applying for employment. Employers need your SSN to help verify your identity and to report your income to the Internal Revenue Service (IRS). Still, you should refrain from providing your SSN until you are at the point of hiring.
- You're opening a financial account. Financial intuitions use SSNs for a variety of reasons. They use the number as a unique way to identify you and to run a credit check. Also, if you are paid money in an account, such as interest, dividends or capital gains, those earnings must be reported to the IRS, and financial institutions need your SSN to do that.
- You're applying for anything that requires a credit check. Examples are credit cards, mobile phone account, utility contract, or rental contract, to name a few.
- Anything that requires a criminal background investigation. In this case, your social security number is used as unique identifier. Many people have the same names, but they don't have the same SSN. It helps differentiate people.

- You're talking with the Social Security Administration or another agency that already has your SSN. However, you should only provide it if you are the one contacting the organization. You should never provide your personal information to someone who has made unsolicited contact with you.
- You are checking your credit report(s). The reporting agencies need your SSN to verify your identity.
- You are enrolling in credit monitoring, creating a fraud alert or freezing your credit reports. (You'll learn more about in this shortly.) Again, they need your SSN to verify your identity and establish the service you request.

Medical offices and social security numbers.

Medical offices got in the practice of using social security numbers to identify patients a long time ago. It was convenient and easy because most everyone knows their social security number and it is a unique identifier that can distinguish us from other patients, especially ones with the same or similar names.

This practice was not really a problem until identity theft, which relies on crooks obtaining your social security number, became an epidemic. When social security numbers became targets, the medical offices that stored patients' social security numbers became vulnerable. Strangely, many offices are nevertheless reluctant to change the practice and continue to use the number as an identifier.

It is up to all of us as patients to protect our information whenever we can, since we can't always rely upon someone else to do it. There are no reliable statistics on how many identity theft cases have resulted from breaches in medical offices, but a good plan of action is not to provide your SSN to the office at all.

As I present to groups around the country on the topic of identity theft, one question always arises: why does my doctor need my social security number? The answer is that they don't. The only exception—for now—is if you have Medicare coverage, in which case, your doctor already has your social security number because it used to be the same as your Medicare number.

In 2015, President Obama signed a law that requires the Department of Health and Human Services (HHS) to provide Medicare enrollees with a Medicare number that is not the enrollee's social security number. The 2015 law, The Medicare Access and CHIP Reauthorization Act, required Centers for Medicare & Medicaid Services (CMS) to remove social security numbers from Medicare cards. As of March 2019, this change has been completed.

The last four numbers of your social security number.

On occasion, you might be asked to verify the last four numbers of your social security number when talking on the phone with organizations about accounts you have with them. This question is being asked to help verify your identity and it cannot be used by itself to obtain your entire SSN. It is perfectly fine to provide these digits. In this case, it is likely that the organization already has your SSN and the person you are talking to on the phone only has the last four digits on a screen in front of them.

Writing your social security number on a check.

NEVER DO THIS! Even though the IRS asks you to do this when submitting a check with your tax return, you should never write your SSN on a check. Your check can be seen by numerous people while it is being processed and you will expose it to all those people, who otherwise would not and should not have access to it.

To illustrate the confusion our government sometimes creates regarding consumer issues, consider the following contradiction. The IRS tells us to write our SSNs on checks submitted to them for tax payments. However, if you go to the website of another government agency, the Federal Trade Commission (FTC), which provides information to consumers about identity theft prevention, they say that you should never write your social security number on a check. In this case, despite the conflicting information, there's a clear right answer. Heed the FTC's advice.

In summary, it's important to protect your social security number as much as possible. Only provide it to someone when the request is legitimate, and it is truly required in order to conduct the transaction. Please keep in mind, however, that your social security number is stored in numerous places where you have no control over how it is protected. For that reason, and because crooks may obtain it despite your best efforts, you should read on to be aware of other steps you can take to protect your identity.

Warning Signs

As explained earlier, identity theft is a very serious problem with the potential for long-term consequences. It's best to prevent identity theft before it occurs, but despite our best efforts, it can happen anyway. If it does, it's best to discover the problem sooner rather than later. In that regard, here are some warning signs that you may have been victimized by one or more identity thieves, and what to do if they appear.

1. You receive a notice that your information was compromised by a data breach at a company where you do business or have an account.

What happened: The organization that sent you the notice had your personal information stolen from them.

What you should do: Freeze all four of your credit reports. How to do this will be discussed shortly.

2. Warning sign: Debt collectors contact you about debts that aren't yours.

What happened: This is sign that someone has obtained loans or credit card accounts in your name.

What you should do: Check all three of your credit reports. Look for any entries that were not caused by your activity. Contact the companies related to the bogus entries.

3. Warning sign: You see withdrawals from your bank account that you can't explain.

What happened: This indicates that someone has obtained your bank login credentials or your account number and routing number.

What you should do: Contact your bank and investigate all transactions to determine their legitimacy.

4. Warning sign: You don't get your bills or other mail.

What happened: Someone has changed your address with the post office or the delivery address for correspondence from the organizations you do business with.

What you should do: Contact the post office and investigate whether someone has changed your address for all your mail. If the post office has not received a change of address form, you should contact all organizations from whom you are no longer receiving mail to advise them of possible fraud with your accounts and to reestablish the correct address.

5. Warning sign: Merchants refuse your checks.

   What happened: Someone is writing checks in your name and has overdrawn your checking account, resulting in the checks being returned to merchants as unpaid.

   What you should do: Contact your bank and look at all check transactions. You may have to close the affected account. Contact the police and report the crime.

6. Warning sign: You find unfamiliar accounts or charges on your credit report.

   What happened: Someone has obtained your personal information and opened financial accounts in your name.

   What you should do: Contact the companies related to the bogus entries and advise them that you are not the one who opened these accounts.

7. Warning sign: Medical providers bill you for services you didn't use, or your health plan rejects your legitimate medical claim because the records show you've reached your benefits limit, or a health plan won't cover you because your medical records show a condition you don't have.

   What happened: Someone has used your identity to obtain medical care.

   What you should do: Contact your health insurance company and advise them of the issue. Contact your primary care physician and advise their office of the situation and of possible false entries in your medical history.

8. Warning sign: The IRS notifies you that more than one tax return was filed in your name, or that you have income from an employer you don't work for.

What happened: Someone has filed a tax return using your identity and/or has used your identity to gain employment.

What you should do: Contact the IRS and the Social Security Administration and let them know you may have been a victim of tax refund fraud and employment fraud.

Besides doing the action noted in each case, there are other, broader actions you need to take to help prevent further fraud.

Checking Your Credit Reports

First, you need to look at all four of your credit reports. That's right, there are four credit reporting agencies, not just the major three (Equifax, Experian and TransUnion) that you probably know. The fourth agency is called Innovis. You can check your credit reports online or by contacting the credit reporting agencies by phone or mail. Here is the information for each agency:

Credit Reporting Bureaus

Equifax: (800) 525-6285
P.O. Box 740241 Atlanta, GA 30374

Experian: (888) 397-3742
P.O. Box 9530 Allen, TX 75013

Jeff Lanza

Innovis: 1-800-540-2505
P.O. Box 1640 Pittsburgh, PA 15230

TransUnion: (800) 680-7289
P.O. Box 2000, Chester, PA 19016

You can contact each agency individually, or by this central online site or phone number:

To order online: www.annualcreditreport.com To order by phone call: 1-877-322-8228

Please note that your credit report at Innovis must be ordered separately, as that company does not participate in the central site. You can pull one credit report per year from each agency for free. So, you shouldn't have to pay for the credit reports unless you have already pulled them within the previous 12 months. Even if you had, if you are the victim of fraud, there should be no charge for your reports.

Be prepared to provide personal information when you pull your credit reports, as it is required to verify your identity and access your information. That includes your social security number. Just make sure that you are providing this information to someone that you contacted, not a person who makes an unsolicited call or sends an email to you. You are initiating this process of checking your credit reports. If you have called the correct number or you are visiting the right website, providing your information should not cause you any problems.

Your Credit Report

Here's a heads-up: Your credit reports are not easy to read or understand. They are made up of a hodge-podge of company names, numbers, credit lines, payment history and more. These figures, at best, are difficult for the lay person to comprehend. Professionals that reveiw your credit reports to decide if they want to loan you money to buy a car for example, are much more skilled at reading them. That's part of their job. But for the rest of us, it's another story.

You should, however, be able to determine if someone has stolen your identity and used it to open new accounts, such as credit card, or obtained a loan in your name.

If this has happened, you will see entries for these accounts indicating that your credit was checked (credit report inquiry) and if the account was opened, there should be a notation of when it was opened, the amount of credit that was issued and history of payment on the debt.

What you are looking for is accounts that you are not familiar with and did not open yourself. For example, let's say you have a credit card issued by "Joe's Big Screen TVs" and that you applied for the credit card when you bought an HDTV six months back. There should be a record of when that credit was issued and how well you are meeting the terms of paying the loan back. That would be a normal entry in your credit report.

If you see that same entry, but you didn't buy a TV at Joe's, or you see any other entry that you did not initiate, you have been a victim of identity theft. The specific type of identity theft here, is called "new account fraud."

What to Do

If you have determined that you are the victim of new account fraud, here is what you need to do:

1. Advise all three credit reporting agencies that this has happened and the specific new accounts that you did not authorize.
2. File a police report about the fraud. This can usually be done over the phone. Ask for a copy of the police report as you will need this for reasons we will discuss shortly.

Next Steps

After you have advised the credit reporting agencies of the fraud and filed a police report, you have three options for your next step. The goal of the next step to prevent further fraud. Here are your choices:

1. **Fraud Alert:** Your credit file at all four credit reporting agencies is flagged for possible identity theft issues. If a potential lender reviewed your credit history and saw the fraud alert, they would not lend money or issue credit unless they made sure it was you that was initiating the transaction. This is a great way to prevent fraud, but fraud alerts only work if the lender pays attention and takes steps to verify the identity of the applicant. (Let's hope they do.) Fraud alerts normally expire after 90 days.

   However, in the case where your identity has already been stolen, the fraud alert will be set to last for seven years. This is called an extended alert. If you choose to place a fraud alert on your credit reports, be sure to ask for an extended alert. Experian, TransUnion and Equifax share information about fraud alerts, so you only have to place a fraud alert with one of the three agencies and that agency will notify the other two. However, a fraud alert on your credit report at Innovis must be place separately.

2. **Credit Report Monitoring:** Your credit files are monitored by a third party - if activity occurs you are notified. There are many companies that provide this service, usually for a monthly fee, which varies widely. Keep in mind that credit monitoring does not prevent the fraud from occurring. The company that you engage to monitor your credit report, if this is your course of action, will only notify you when there is activity in your credit report. It could be real-time notification through an email or a phone call, but it may not be fast enough to prevent the account(s) from being opened in the first place. The credit monitoring companies advertise that they will help you resolve the situation if you have been a victim of identity theft and that is great service. But credit monitoring, by itself, does not prevent the fraud.

3. **Credit Report Freeze:** A total lockdown of new account activity in your name and a proven way to protect against identity theft. Freezing prevents third parties from accessing your credit report, with some exceptions.

   To explain, let's take a hypothetical example. A crook obtains your social security number and other information about you and attempts to open a credit card account in your name. The credit card company will run a credit check on you (because your identity is being used) before the credit card is issued in your name, to the crook. If your credit report is frozen, the credit card company cannot get access to your credit report. If they can't see your reports, they will not approve the credit card application. You might see that freezing your credit reports is a rock-solid way to prevent further fraud if you have been a victim of identity theft. Even if you have not been victimized, freezing your reports can be used to prevent fraud from occurring preemptively. You don't have to be a victim of identity theft to freeze your credit reports, anyone can do it.

On September 21, 2018, the Economic Growth, Regulatory Relief, and Consumer Protection Act went into effect nationwide. The law makes it free to freeze your credit reports for residents of all 50 states. Previously, residents of some states were required to pay to freeze their reports.

Lifting freezes

If your credit report is frozen, you will not be able to have your credit checked for your own legitimate purposes, such as when you open a new credit card account or apply for a car loan. In this circumstance, you can temporarily lift the freeze with a PIN (personal identification number) that you will receive when you freeze it. You will receive four separate PINs, one for each of the four frozen credit reports. It is extremely important that you protect the PINs, but still have them handy when it comes time to lift the freezes. Without the PINs, it can be a gigantic hassle to lift the freezes, which could involve a lot of paperwork and documentation to prove your identity. The new law makes it free to lift credit report freezes.

Freezes and current credit cards

Placing a security freeze on your credit won't affect how you use your current credit accounts. Any credit cards or other accounts you currently have will continue to function as before.

Freezes and minors

It is important to protect minors from identity theft. Imagine if a minor had credit cards opened in their name. They could be victimized for years before they become aware that it has happened. Besides making credit freezes free for adults in all 50 states, the new federal law also allows parents and guardians to freeze the credit reports of children who are 15 years-of-age or under.

You might be thinking that minors don't have credit reports to freeze. Your thinking would be correct. Minors should not have a credit report. If they do, they have already been victimized and in this case, you should contact the credit reporting agencies to let them know that a minor's identity may have been used for fraud.

If a minor does not have a credit report, all is good. The new law allows you to create a credit report for a minor and freeze it immediately. This action is highly recommended to protect children from many types of identity theft. Again, save the PINs!

The Equifax breach

If I were to borrow a phrase to describe a major cyber breach, September 7th, 2017 was "a day that will live in infamy." This is the day that we learned that Equifax, one of the major credit reporting agencies, had a computer breach that resulted in the personal information of over 148 million Americans being put at risk. The personal information included social security numbers, which could be used to steal a person's identity. More recently, on March 7, 2019, the CEO of Equifax appeared before Congress to answer questions about the breach. He was sharply rebuked by members of Congress for the seriousness of the breach and lax security which allowed the breach to occur. (Even though he was not CEO at the time of the breach.) Since the breach involved social security numbers which could be used by a criminal to steal a victim's identity and open new accounts in their name, it is important to take preventative steps. The best of these steps is to freeze all four of your credit reports.

Chapter Summary

Identity theft can be highly profitable crime for the criminals. Three common types of identity theft are new account fraud, tax refund fraud and medical identity theft. The victims can have their lives turned upside down by the time-consuming, hassled-filled experience of repairing their good name. This chapter has described the most common ways identity theft occurs and what specific actions you can take to prevent it from occurring and what to do if you become a victim.

The most important thing is to protect your social security number. If you think it may be in the hands of someone who might use it for fraud, the best thing to do is to freeze all four credit reports for you and family members, including children. Utilizing services that monitor your credit reports and other accounts may also be used to help alert you to fraud and help you resolve it.

What to Shred and How to Shred it

Shredding is an important way to prevent people from obtaining sensitive information from your trash, but what should you shred?

Don't worry about paper with just your name and address on it. You don't need to shred magazine covers and envelopes. Your name and address can be obtained in many places.

Do shred financial statements, anything containing account numbers, birthdates, or social security numbers. Credit card offers or other solicitations for financial accounts should be shredded.

What kind of shredder?

There are three secure options:

1. cross-cut
2. diamond-cut
3. micro-cut shredder

Don't use a strip-cut shredder, which is not secure.

If you are holding many documents that are too voluminous to shred at home, look for local businesses that advertise shred days. Just keep those documents secure until you take them to be shredded.

Jeff Lanza

Chapter 3
Emotions

"Common sense is not so common."

Voltaire

Shortly after I began my career as an FBI agent in the Bureau's Kansas City Division, I heard an interesting recounting of a conversation that two mobsters had on a phone line that was wiretapped by the FBI. The mobsters, who I will call Tony and Joe, had this conversation while an FBI agent listened to the wiretap:

Tony: Joe, I am really glad you called.

Joe: Yeah, why?

Tony: I got a little problem. I think the FBI is tapping my phone.

Joe: What are you going to do about it?

Tony: I already got it taken care of. I got a new number.

Joe: OK, good. Gimme the number.

Tony: I better not give it to you on the phone. I'll meet you for lunch and give it to you then.

Joe: I can't meet you for lunch.

Tony: OK, I'll give it to you now on the phone…but better give you the number…backwards.

Joe: Good idea.

Tony proceeded to give him the number backwards. The FBI, of course, sent the backwards number to its cryptology department immediately. Six months later, using state of the art, super computers, we had the new number!

This short exchange between Tony and Joe illustrates how important the role of common sense is when it comes to everyday occurrences. As it relates to fraud, the use of common sense by a target for fraud may stop victimization before it occurs.

In many cases where fraud occurs, the perpetrator attempts to manipulate the victim into making an emotional decision, which helps grease the wheels for the crime to occur. When we make decisions based on emotion rather than on common sense, there is a greater chance that we will make an unwise decision.

Common examples of this manipulation include a phone call made by a person who purports to be from the Internal Revenue Service who claims you owe back taxes; a phone call from a person who says they are from "software support" and alleging that your computer has been infected with a virus; or a person who calls on the phone indicating that they are a grandchild in trouble. If contact is made via email or text message, the communication may contain words like "fraud alert" or "your account has been compromised."

These situations have the potential to elicit an emotional reaction from the person receiving the call. Emotions motivate us to want to solve the problem as quickly as possible. This usually involves providing money, personal information, access to a computer, or all of the above.

If logic and common sense prevailed in these interactions, the result might be very different. The potential victim might stop and think about the veracity of the information. It is true that people owe the IRS money, computers get infected with viruses, grandchildren get in trouble, and online accounts get compromised. However, if any of these things happen in our lives, before we have an emotional reaction, we must determine through logic and common sense if what is alleged to be happening is true and, if so, what the appropriate steps are to take if this is the case.

Let's look at the examples mentioned above through the lenses of emotion versus logic and common sense.

IRS scam phone call

There are variations on this scam, but most often, the potential victim receives a phone call (also referred to as a "robocall," which is short for "robot call"). If the call is answered or picked up by an answering machine, a computer-generated voice will tell you that you are being sued by the IRS for back taxes owed. Here is a transcript of a call that I received of this nature:

"The reason for this call is the IRS, Internal Revenue Service, is filing lawsuit against you. To get more information about this case file, please call immediately on our department number."

The number is provided, and if the target calls it, they will be connected to a person who has been trained in the fine art of scamming people, mostly through the subtle and not-so-subtle manipulation of their emotions. The scammer will tell the target that they are behind on their taxes, and if they don't pay right away, they will be arrested by government agents. If people don't resist this attempt to circumvent logic and common sense, they might follow the scammer's instructions to obtain store gift cards or pre-paid debit cards and then read the numbers on these cards to the scammer. In effect, this transfers the money paid for the cards to the scammers.

Let's look at how a person might respond emotionally versus logically.

Emotion: I owe money to a powerful government agency. Do I really want to be arrested? If that happens, I won't be able to pay the money I owe, and they might keep me in jail indefinitely.

Logic and common sense: If you owe the IRS money, they notify you by U.S. mail before any phone calls that might be made to you directly. If you have not received any of these letters, you probably don't owe them money. And even if you did, the IRS will not accept payment in the form of a pre-paid debit card or gift card.

Your computer has been hacked

This is according to the unsolicited phone call you receive, of course. The caller may claim that they are from a software company such as Microsoft, and that they have become aware of a breach on your computer. "Hacked" can mean different things, but most likely the scenario involves the scammer helping you rid your computer of a virus. To accomplish this feat, they want you to provide them with remote access to your computer. There are legitimate reasons why you might provide remote access to your computer to a third party, but it is NOT appropriate when an unsolicited caller wants to have this access.

Many nasty things can happen if you provide remote computer access to a scammer. First, to gain this access, the scammer will instruct you to download software from a website which will facilitate the remote access. Once this happens, the scammer will control your computer from afar. If you are looking at their computer screen, you can watch some of what is happening in real time. The scammer will act like they are helping you, but in reality, they may be secretly stealing information or downloading viruses to your computer, which is ironic, because they claim to be helping to eliminate viruses!

Then, without hesitation, the scammer will ask you to pay for their "virus removal services." Once a payment is made, you essentially will have been scammed twice in one phone call.

Again, let's look at how a person might respond emotionally versus logically.

Emotion: Your computer is infected with malware. This could be a big problem which needs my immediate attention.

Logic and common sense: How would someone know that your computer has been infected with a virus, unless it's not a person but your antivirus software, which might notify with a message on your computer, but not by phone call. There are no people standing by watching your computer, ready to jump into action.

Grandparent scam

This scam starts with two preconceptions: first, that a grandparent will come to the aid of a grandchild in a time of crisis, and second, that most grandparents don't live with their grandchildren, so they are not always aware of their whereabouts. The scam starts with a phone call from the scammer to the target. The target's name and phone number can be easily obtained through public records. In some cases, the scammers might use social media to start their search and get preliminary information about targets and their grandchildren, including names. For this reason, it is important not to accept social media connections or friend requests from anyone that you don't know. The amount of information that a scammer can obtain is limited when there is no connection.

In the simplest case, the scammer will obtain a target's name and phone number from public records. They will look for names that were more popular during the years when today's potential grandparent was born, such as Dorothy, Helen, Margaret, George, Edward, and Ronald. The scammers know that there is a higher chance that these names belong to those born in the 1920s and 1930s. According to the Social Security Administration, these six names were the some of the most popular names for girls and boys born in those two decades.

The scammer will begin with one of these names and start dialing. Here is an example of an exchange between a scammer and a caller, which is based on a real story:

Target: Hello. Scammer: Grandpa? Target: Randy?

Scammer: Yeah.

Target: What's the matter?

Scammer: I've been in a car wreck. Target: Are you okay?

Scammer: Yeah, but I need some money.

The scammer then instructed the target to send money to help resolve the situation. In this case the "situation" was a car accident, but there are many variations on this scam.

Another common story involves the grandchild having been arrested and in need of bail money. In any case, the scammer always instructs the target not to tell his or her parents and to only call back on the number the scammer is calling from because they lost their cell phone or because the battery is dead. Of course, if the target called their actual grandchild back on their known number, they would discover that their grandchild has not been in an accident or arrested, and that the whole thing is a scam.

Once more, emotion versus logic.

Emotion: A grandchild is hurt or in trouble. An emotional reaction to the set of circumstances that a scammer has put forth may cause the target to immediately act. They may do what their grandchild says and ask questions later.

Logic and common sense: If a grandchild really needs your help, wouldn't they want their parents involved as well? Wouldn't the grandchild have their cell phone available for a call back? In any case, it always makes sense to verify the identity of a caller, even if it sounds like it might be a grandchild. Call them back at a number you know to be theirs and talk to them before sending any money.

In the Internet Age, it can be easy to get tricked online or on the phone by having a scammer manipulate our emotions. In examples described above, the scammer may have used the internet to identify victims or make robocalls. One of our best defenses against fraud is logic and common sense. When a situation involves providing information, money, or access to anyone, ask yourself, "Does this situation make sense?" It is especially important to do this when you have received the contact unsolicited (as opposed to initiating it yourself). Ask questions, take steps to determine the truthfulness of the claim, and don't let emotions drive your behavior.

A Victim's Story

Following a recent presentation, a member of the audience told me that his mother received a phone call from a person claiming to be a grandchild who had been arrested for fishing without a license. He asked the victim not to tell other family members about the arrest and to wire transfer $2,000 so he could pay a fine. He told her specifically how to wire the money using the services of a local retailer. After sending the money, the victim received another phone call from the man, who claimed that his friend was also arrested for the same infraction. Following the caller's instructions, the victim sent another $2,000 by wire transfer. A brief time later, the victim found out that her grandchild had not been arrested or fishing. In fact, the grandchild was at his home just a few miles from the victim. An emotional reaction caused the victim to respond to the phone call and send money both times without telling any family members, as instructed by the crook.

Jeff Lanza

Chapter 4
Malware

"The problem of viruses is temporary and will be solved in two years."

John McAfee, 1988

The word "malware" is derived from two terms: "malicious" and "software." Software is what operates the hardware, or physical components, of your computer. Malicious—well, you probably know what that means. Hateful, spiteful, mean, nasty, mischievous, and, well, you get the idea. It does bad things to your computer, or makes your computer do bad things. Malware is wide-ranging enough to be categorized. Here are a few categories of malware:

Virus – Designed to disrupt legitimate programs on your computer. It has the ability to replicate itself.

Spyware – Software that may take information from your computer without your knowledge and sends it to others.

Worm – Software that does not alter files but duplicates itself in active computer memory and affects your ability to use your computer.

Trojan horse – Computer code that may be hidden in another program. When the program is run, the malicious software installs itself on the victim's computer.

Keylogger – A program that records the keystrokes on the victim's computer keyboard. The information can be sent to another person who may use it to log in to a victim's online accounts.

Screen capture – A program that takes snapshots or "captures" of your computer screen and sends them to the hackers. The program can allow the hackers to see the various websites you are visiting. Used in combination with keylogger, it can give the hackers everything they need to steal login credentials to your accounts.

Cryptolocker – A program that can encrypt or lock all of the files on a computer. It is usually used to extort victims for a ransom payment to unlock the files.

Camfecting malware – This is a software program that has a specific ability to turn on your webcam, allowing a hacker to peer at you or anyone who in the room where your computer is located. Some of the programs can activate the webcam without triggering the light that indicates the webcam is turned on.

Scareware – Software that causes messages to appear on your computer indicating that your computer is infected with malware. It is infected, by the scareware, but the hackers are not referring to that. They falsely claim there is an infection that they can fix if you pay them money.

There are a few different ways you can get malware on your computer. Many times, it involves clicking on links, attachments, or emails that surreptitiously download it to your computer. Once this happens, bad things can occur. For example, in the case of keystroke logging, the malware records keystrokes as the victim types them. It may have the capability to send them to the hackers. If these keystrokes are the usernames and passwords to your online accounts, the hackers may then have the credentials needed to log in to those accounts. How do they know what sites you were logging into? With screen capture malware. Both screen capture and keylogger work in the background and you have no idea it's even happening. It does not affect your ability to log in to your accounts; you can still do that. But so can the hackers, because they will have your login credentials that were stolen by the keylogging software!

In many cases, the delivery system for malware is through emails. To avoid malware delivered through email, your best defense is to not click on links or attachments in emails that fall into these categories:

Emails from unknown senders. Here is a simple rule. If you receive an email from someone whose name you don't recognize, don't click on a link or attachment in that email.

Emails that look suspicious. If you receive an email from someone you know but all it contains is a link, don't click on the link. It is likely, under this circumstance, that the email account of the sender has been compromised. The hackers may be trying to use the hijacked email account to spread malware.

Emails that don't make sense. Before clicking on a link or attachment in an email, ask yourself a key question: does this email make sense? For example, I received an email in which the sender was listed as "The Internal Revenue Service." The contents of the email indicated that my taxes from a previous year were in "arrears." There was an attachment in the email labeled "calculations" and instructions in the email to open that attachment.

Of course, an email like this may elicit an emotional reaction from the receiver, who may think they owe the IRS some money. But if you stop and think about it, the email itself doesn't make sense. If you really do owe money to the IRS, their first notification to you is not going to come in the form of an email. It will be physical mail delivered by the U.S. Postal Service. Your notification will not be in the form of a text message, Facebook update, Tweet, Snapchat photo, Vine video, or email!

If the email you are reading doesn't make sense, don't click on anything in the email.

Besides using emails to infect victims' computers with malware, hackers use other techniques.

Malware bundled with other software. Sometimes you may opt to download software to a computer from a website.

The software you seek may be legitimate and serve a desired purpose. However, you should only download software from a legitimate vendor's site and make sure you know exactly what you are installing. Uncheck any boxes offering to download extra programs with your desired program. Don't just click "OK" throughout the download process. Carefully inspect what you are agreeing to and don't agree to anything except the software you wanted in the first place.

Peer-to-peer networks. Websites that allow you to share files with other user's computers have known issues with spreading malware. Avoid these sites. If there are people in your family who use peer-to-peer networks, do not use the same computer that they do for sensitive tasks like online banking or even email. It would be best to have a separate computer used only for peer-to-peer activities, if you must use them at all.

Infected websites. Sometimes legitimate websites may become compromised. In this case, visitors to these sites may unknowingly have their computers infected just by visiting the sites, which can take advantage of known vulnerabilities on your computer. We have no control over the security of the websites we visit. But we do have control over our own computers' security. Your best defense here is to keep your all of your software updated, which will reduce your vulnerabilities.

Infected removable drives. Sometimes devices we plug into our computer can contain malware. These devices include portable hard drives and USB flash drives. Your best defense is to disable auto-run features for these devices. This can be done in your computer's settings. If you do plug a device into your computer, you should run a malware scan with your antivirus software before any programs can run from the drive.

There are many ways (or, as security professionals say, "vectors") for a malware attack. Your best defense for each threat vector has been described above. Besides those specific defenses, it is important that computers be protected with a general antivirus program that is kept up to date. There are many brand names in the antivirus market. There are free versions and paid versions. Generally, it has not been proven that any one brand works better at defending your computer than another, nor that the free versions are less secure. However, paid versions of antivirus programs usually offer more features that could provide more protection under certain circumstances.

If you have a Windows PC, you might also consider the antivirus program that is included with Microsoft Vista and versions 7, 8.1, and 10. It is provided for free. It is called Windows Defender and it is included in the Windows Essentials software. (You may have to download it, depending on your version of Microsoft's operating system.)

If you happen to own a Mac, be advised that Apple computers are not immune to malware and users should use protective software for these products.

Remember, antivirus programs are not infallible, but they are our first line of defense and create a perimeter shield against hackers. Because of their fallibility, you do need additional protection. What is the additional protection, you ask? You. It's your vigilance, and it's your behavior online. Avoid risk, be careful, and keep your computer secure.

Jeff Lanza

Chapter 5
Phishing

An actuary can tell you how many people between the ages of 50 and 60 will die this year. A Sicilian actuary will tell you their names.

Actuarial science uses the laws of probability and statistics to predict the possibility of things happening in the future. Much of the predictability depends on the size of the group under consideration. Generally, the larger the group, the more accurate the predictions become.

When it comes to phishing, larger numbers also work to the scammers' advantage. A greater number of phishing emails sent means a greater number of victims hooked.

Before I go on about phishing, let's take a step back and talk about what phishing is and how it works. The term "phishing" first appeared around 1995 and it pertained to computer scammers' attempts to catch people in an online scam of one sort or another. Webster's Dictionary defines phishing this way:

"A scam by which an e-mail user is duped into revealing personal or confidential information which the scammer can use illicitly."

Phishing can be defined more broadly than this, as phishing can also be undertaken over the phone or in person. The concept of phishing relates to fishing in a lake or ocean. A person that's fishing knows that casting a line or net will not catch all the fish in the water. But because there are a lot of fish targets, if that person fishes correctly, they are likely to catch a few.

Phishing emails

Many people have asked me why they received an email from a bank that they don't use or had never even heard of. The answer is based on the concept of email phishing. Scammers send out large numbers of emails designed to look as if they are coming from a certain bank. They know that the emails will land in the email accounts of people who are not customers of that bank, but it doesn't matter because the fake email will also be received by people who do bank there. When the email reaches its target and a recipient falls for the phishing scam, they might be tricked into providing their bank login credentials to the scammers. (This is called a bank account takeover. There is a separate chapter focused on this crime.)

Telephone phishing

Telephones, both land line and mobile, are another ripe conduit for phishing by crooks. Phishing is most often used over the phone in cases where the caller is requesting money, information, or access to a person's computer. Common examples include fake calls from the IRS, Microsoft, or a person claiming to be a grandchild in trouble.

The scammer/caller knows that many people receiving these calls will either not answer, hang up after answering, or not be scammed at all. The scammer knows that they are not going to catch every "fish" in the sea. But all they need is for a few victims to fall for the trick to get a nice return. In short, if they put out their line enough times, they will get a "catch."

How to avoid phishing attempts

There is a very simple strategy to prevent phishing scammers from victimizing you:

BEWARE OF UNSOLICITED COMMUNICATION AND DON'T TAKE INSTRUCTIONS FROM THOSE WHO HAVE CONTACTED YOU THIS WAY UNLESS YOU HAVE VERIFIED THEIR LEGITMACY.

Let's take some of the examples of scams discussed in the chapter about emotions and discuss how you might go about responding.

Scam:

You receive a phone call from someone claiming to be from the Internal Revenue Service, who tells you that you are behind on your tax payments and if you don't pay right away, you will be arrested by government agents.

Response:

If it is a recording on your answering machine, do not call the number provided. If, rather than a listening to a recorded message, you are talking to a person claiming to be with the IRS, do not engage them in conversation and discontinue the phone call as soon as possible. In other words, hang up. The longer you engage, the greater the chance they could trick you. One person told me that they were not convinced by a caller claiming that they were with the IRS until the caller provided an IRS badge number to her. Really? A crook can't make up a number on the spot? Also, don't toy with callers because you know the call is a scam. The scammers may try to inundate you with future calls to punish you.

If you have caller ID, disregard the number associated with the call. With technology, it is very easy to spoof a phone number to make appear as though an incoming call is coming from a number other than the real one. A crook can look up the number of the IRS and make it appear as the incoming caller's number.

By the way, if you do have an issue with unpaid taxes, as mentioned previously in this book, the IRS will notify you by mail before you receive a phone call. If you have any concern that you owe money to the IRS, then look up their phone number and call the agency yourself using that number.

One final note on this scam: should you report the attempted scam to authorities? Don't bother. Neither the IRS nor a law enforcement agency is going to take any action if you have not lost money to the scammers. If you did provide money to the scammers, then you should report the crime to the police and the IRS, but in most cases, it will just be added to the statistics of those who have been tricked before you, which, according to the federal government, number in the thousands of victims and hundreds of million dollars in losses.

Scam:

A caller claims that your computer is infected with malware. They want remote access to your computer to fix the problem. This is called a tech support scam.

Response:

Hang up the phone. It is not possible for an unsolicited caller to know anything about your computer. As with the fake IRS call, even if you know it's a scam, you should not engage with the caller or try to have fun with them. You may end up getting more calls, which is no fun at all.

It should be noted that computers do have issues that sometimes need to be resolved by calling customer support. In some cases, the support specialist may ask you for your permission to obtain remote access to your computer, as this is the most efficient way to fix an issue in most cases. It is acceptable to provide this access when you have placed the phone call to a number that you have looked up yourself and you know that it is the correct number for the company whose support you seek.

Scam:

A caller claims to be a grandchild in trouble. Of course, this scam only applies to people who have grandchildren, more specifically, with grandchildren old enough to get in the kind of trouble that would require a grandparent's help. Common scenarios include a grandchild who has been arrested and needs bail money or a grandchild that has been in a car accident and needs to pay a medical bill.

In any case, the "grandchild" tells the grandparent not to tell their parents and not to call them back. The caller will give the victim specific instructions on how to wire transfer money or to buy merchant gift cards or pre-paid debit cards. They will then ask the grandparent to provide the "grandchild" with the gift card number, which in effect transfers the money to the scammer.

Response:

The following advice is true no matter how much the caller may sound like a grandchild, even if the caller knows the name of your grandchild. The scammer may have obtained the name through social media or another source, or the victim may have inadvertently given the name to the caller without realizing.

After hanging up the phone, contact the grandchild that is supposedly in trouble at a phone number that you know belongs to them, even if you have been told not to call. You must verify the caller's identity before providing money. You can also establish a passphrase or code word with grandchildren that they should use if they really do need your help.

Some have suggested that the grandparent should ask a question or two to which only an actual grandchild would know the answer. I wouldn't recommend this strategy by itself, as a scammer can obtain lots of background information about a target on social media sites.

There is more information about these scams in other parts of the book, but I would like to close this chapter with a story about how to not become a victim of phishing. This story involves the phone, but the lesson also applies to email phishing attempts. The best way to stay safe is to always verify the identity of the person to whom you are communicating.

So, here is a very personal story that relates to that point.

I joined the FBI in 1988, and in July of that year I arrived at my first office assignment in Kansas City, Missouri. I was assigned to a white-collar crime squad, and one Friday afternoon in September 1988, an agent from our organized crime squad came over to the white-collar area. "Anybody want to go on a search warrant on Sunday morning?" he asked. "We need another person."

As a new agent, I wanted to do everything, so I was quick to respond. "Sure, I'll go," I answered.

Two days later, the agent and I arrived at the home of a bookie and served the warrant, which allowed us to take any property believed to be connected to illegal gambling. I was at the bookie's desk gathering the evidence, while the other agent was interviewing the bookie in another room.

It was a Sunday morning during football season, so something happened that one might expect at a bookie's desk: the phone rang. I was a new agent and not sure if I should just let it ring or not, so I asked the other agent. "Go ahead and answer it," he said.

Before I tell you what transpired next, I must digress. My father was a small business owner in Norwalk, Connecticut. He owned a Hallmark Card store and a convenience store that was named Jet Variety. As a teenager, I helped my dad around the store after school, on weekends, and during summers. On occasion, a group of men would congregate in the store after buying a newspaper called The New York Post. This paper was very popular among the men because it had an extensive sports section. Included in this section were the betting lines for games taking place on any given day. The men would come into the store on a regular basis, grab the paper, and talk to each other about what games they were going to bet on that day with their bookie. There were many occasions over the years when I overheard these men's conversations, and I started to learn about the meaning of the betting lines. Over time, I learned the vernacular and the parlance of gambling by listening to these men.

Now, jump back forward to the bookie's house in 1988. I was at the bookie's desk wearing my gun and badge, gathering the betting records in fulfillment of the terms of the court-ordered search warrant. When I asked the agent what to do about the ringing phone, he told me to answer it. I did.

I answered the phone as I would have under normal circumstances. "Hello."

"Who is this?" The caller asked.

"Jeff." I was not acting in an undercover capacity, so I told him my real name.

"This is Mike," he said. "Hey Mike."

"What is the spread on the Chiefs today?" Mike asked.

I knew exactly what to tell him because the bookie's paperwork was right in front of me. I knew how to read the lines because it was part of the jargon the men used in my dad's store.

"The Chiefs are plus 6 ½," I told him, reading directly from the bookie's sheet.

"OK, gimme fifty on the Chiefs," Mike instructed.

"You got it. Anything else, Mike?" I asked, jotting down his bet.

"That's it for now," he replied.

I went back to making an inventory of the bookie's papers when the phone rang again. "Who's this?" the caller asked. A pattern was starting to develop.

"Jeff. Who's this?" "Frank."

"Hey Frank, what can I do for you?" I asked. "What's the over on the Vikings?" Frank asked.

Remembering this terminology from listening to the guys in my dad's store, I looked for the Vikings on the bookie's sheet and saw the number indicating the total number of points a bettor thought would be scored by both teams together. The bettor could place a bet the final score would be under or over that number.

"Forty-four," I told him.

"Give me the over for twenty-five," Frank said. "You got it, Frank," I said.

"Thanks Jeff," Frank said.

This went on for about an hour and no one asked why the regular bookie wasn't answering the phone. That is, no one except the FBI agent at our office downtown who was listening to the bookie's phone, as our wiretap on it was still active. I was so new in the office that he didn't even know my name. "I was wondering what the hell was going on! Two FBI agents go in and bust the bookie, and then some other bookie named Jeff starts taking bets," he told me later. "You sounded like a real bookie."

The agent might have been wondering about me, but the bettors didn't. Mostly, they just wanted to get their bets placed. One bettor was also concerned that he might not be able to collect from me if he won his bet. "Jeff, I don't know you," the bettor said. "But I get paid on Tuesdays. You are still gonna pay me, right?"

"Yeah, don't worry about it." I said.

"OK. I just want to be sure." He then went on to tell me his name, spelling his last name out letter by letter, followed by his address, with the street also spelled out. "You're gonna come over on Tuesday, right?" he asked.

"Oh, don't worry. We'll be over," I said.

A little later a bettor called who was more circumspect than the previous callers. "Who's this?" he asked.

"Jeff."

"Jeff who?" the caller asked.

I really wasn't that comfortable in this impromptu undercover role as a bookie. His question put me on the spot. I didn't want to give him my last name and I wasn't quick enough to make something up. I told him the truth. "Jeff with the FBI," I said.

After saying that, I thought I would hear a click on the other end of the phone line. Instead, I heard hearty laughter. "Jeff with the FBI. That's really funny, Jeff with the FBI," he said, cracking up. "OK, Jeff WITH THE FBI! I want a hundred on the Chiefs," he ordered, still laughing.

My time as an FBI bookie came to an end after about two hours of taking bets. What I learned from that experience was that I really didn't think I could be an effective undercover agent. In this situation, I mostly told the truth. But in a real undercover case, I would have to learn to be deceptive and think quickly in potentially dangerous situations. I decided to leave the undercover work to someone else.

As it relates to phishing, it is important to make sure you know the identity of the person with whom you are communicating. Of all the people I spoke to that day as an "FBI bookie," only one caller tried to verify my identity. Maybe it had to do with the fact that they were the ones making the phone call at a number they knew to be for their bookie.

For all of us that receive contact, it is important to always to verify the identity of the communicator before we provide money, information, or access to personal property.

Jeff Lanza

Chapter 6
Ransomware

"I remember the time I was kidnapped and they sent a piece of my finger to my father. He said he wanted more proof."

Rodney Dangerfield

In the 1920s and 1930s, hoodlums, to generate income, kidnapped people and held them for ransom. To advise the victims' families of their demands, they would write a ransom note. To expedite the process of writing a ransom note and to avoid duplicating effort over multiple kidnappings, one hoodlum, Verne Sankey, prepared a fill-in- the-blank ransom note. It contained such terms as "we are holding   for Sixty Thousand Dollars." It was like a template you might find today on the internet for a writing business correspondence: just fill in the blanks to personalize the communication to your specific situation.

Today, it would be very unusual to see a person kidnapped and held for ransom (in the United States, at least). Instead, we are experiencing a growing amount of a different kind of kidnapping, wherein the internet is used to facilitate the crime.

The FBI reported that, in 2016 alone, Americans handed over one billion dollars to hackers as ransom payments. But who or what was being held hostage that required ransom payment to release? It was the computer files on the victims' own computers. The hackers didn't kidnap or steal the files, they just encrypted them with malware so the victims couldn't access them. Only the hackers had the encryption keys to unlock the files. Without them, the victims would never see their files again. On the other hand, if they paid up, the victims got the encryption key to unlock their files. So, they paid, in 2016 alone, about one billion dollars to hackers. This crime not only continues today but is growing to be a much more serious problem.

To begin to understand the crime of ransomware and how it works, we need to address the concept of encryption. Encryption is a method of scrambling a message so it becomes unreadable. The only way to then read the message is by decrypting it with a key. Unless you have the key, it is impossible to decipher it. Encryption is not a new thing, of course—it has been used for centuries. In wartime, for example, messages were encrypted to prevent them from being read if they fell into enemy hands.

Today, however, hackers have found a way to victimize us via our computers, using encryption technology and the old-fashioned technique of holding something valuable for ransom.

```
                    To whom it may concern

Do not notify police, If you do, and theystart making it not
for us, you will never see_____alive again.
We are holding_____ for Sixty Thousand Dollars,
We are asking you to get this money in Ten and Twenty dollar
bills and they must be old bills only.
  When you get this money ready and are willing to pay as above
for the safe return of _____, then insert the following add
in the Denver Post, personal items.

             ( Please write, I am ready to return )
                    sign ( mabel )


Now we want you to understand that we are not going to take
any chance of being captured wile closing this deal, so you
can take up your mind here and now that you will either pay
the above, or that _____ will never be returned.
Keep all of my letters as they must all be returned to me with
the money.
We will not stand for any stalling thru advise that police
may give you.
You are smart enough to know what the results will be if you
try that.
You know what happended to little Charles Lindberg through his
 father calling the police' He would be alive today if his
father had followed instructions given him.
You are to choose one of these to courses,Either insert add
and be prepared to pay ransome, Or fogget it all.
```

Fill-in-the-blank ransom note from the 1930s.

Source: National Archives

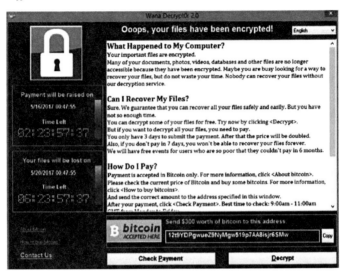

Ransomware note from a 2017 attack.
Source: FBI

The name for this is ransomware. It's today's version of kidnapping. In reality, there is no actual "kidnapping" of your information. You still have it, since it resides on your computer and was never absconded with at all. However, the information, such as your documents, pictures and other files, are encrypted and rendered unreadable by you or anyone else who doesn't have the encryption key. Guess who has the encryption key? The hackers, of course. And what do they want before they give you the decryption key? Your money, of course. How much they demand depends on who the victim is. For a business, it could be thousands of dollars or more. For an individual, the ransom demand is usually about $500. Want to see your family photos that you uploaded to your computer alive again? Pay the ransom. Want to see your spreadsheets? Pay the ransom. Want to see your stored letters? Pay the ransom.

Ransomware has reached epidemic proportions, and it only seems to be getting worse. In May 2017, a ransomware attack dubbed "Wannacry" hit thousands of computers in over 100 countries. Much of the effect was felt by the business community. Organizations are particularly vulnerable to ransomware, as their computer files are needed to operate their business.

Ransomware starts when a victim opens an email sent to them by hackers. In most cases, just opening the email will not do anything to the victim's computer. However, if the victim clicks on a link or an attachment in the email, a ransomware attack can occur.

The demand for payment, or ransom note, appears on your computer screen, delivered through the malware that resides on your computer. If you become a victim of this type of cyber fraud, you have a few choices:

1. Pay the ransom and hope you get the decryption key. I say "hope" because there is no guarantee that the hackers will follow through on their promise to give you the key. In most cases, however, the hackers will give you the key because they want to maintain their reputation for excellent customer service. (What's next, a customer satisfaction survey? "How was your hacking experience with us? Click on the smiley face or frowny face.") The FBI does not recommend that anyone pay ransom in cases like this because, for one thing, it emboldens the hackers. The money that you pay might be used to fund other criminal activities as well. But, in truth, paying may be your only option if you have no other way to recover your files.

2.   Thumb your nose at the hackers and refuse to pay on principle, or for any other reason. In this case, you may never get your files unlocked.

3.   Contact a computer professional and see if there is any way they can decrypt your files without obtaining the key from the hackers. In some cases, this may be possible, depending on the type of encryption that was used to lock up your files.

4.   Recover your files from an unencrypted backup. This is your best option and it guarantees that you can recover your files without paying a ransom. However, there is one caveat: you need to have backed up your files. If there is one thing that people are complacent about, it's keeping a current backup. You can back up to a hard drive or flash drive that is connected to the computer. If you use this option, it's a good idea to disconnect when you are not backing up. If your back up drive is connected all of the time, it, your backup files on this drive could also be encrypted by malware at the time of an original infection. Back up to the hard drive and then disconnect it.

Another option for back up is in the cloud. These services are generally considered secure and may provide protection against ransomware. In most cases you should be able to recover your files from the cloud in the event of a ransomware attack.

You might be wondering why law enforcement doesn't go after and catch the people or groups behind the ransomware attacks. There are two reasons why there has not been an effective law enforcement response to the ransomware epidemic. The first has to do how the money is transferred to the crooks when victims pay the ransom. In most cases, the ransom is demanded in the virtual currency Bitcoin. Its use by the hackers renders traditional law enforcement techniques for following the money ineffectual.

The second reason is that even if law enforcement could follow the money to the hackers, they can't arrest them. It is believed that most cases of ransomware originate outside of the United States, and U.S. authorities would need the cooperation of the countries where the hackers live to arrest and prosecute them. Law enforcement doesn't often get that cooperation.

In short, it's been difficult to stop the hackers involved in ransomware attacks. Ultimately, the solution lies with the victims and potential victims, who are all of us. The answer lies with prevention—namely, two simple things we can all do to stop ransomware from infiltrating our lives.

First, it's key to stop a ransomware infection before it starts, by being careful where you click. As discussed previously, don't click on links or attachments in suspicious emails, those from unknown senders, or emails that don't make sense. Second, back up your computer files on a regular basis either on a hard drive or flash drive. Disconnect it after you have finished backing up. Cloud back up is another option.

If we take preventative steps to make sure we are not victimized by ransomware, we will render the crooks' business model ineffective. A lack of profit from the crime will cause the crime itself to dry up and go away.

Jeff Lanza

Chapter 7
Bank Account Takeovers

Bank robber Willie Sutton was reported as to have said, when a reporter asked why he robbed banks, "Because that's where the money is!"

Willie denied it and said that the quote was made up by the reporter.

An account takeover happens when a hacker gains control of an online account. Examples include email accounts, social media accounts, and financial accounts like those of credit cards and banks. In short, any online account for which you have registered by creating a username and password could be a target if it provides value to a hacker. In most cases, hackers want to use the access to transfer money from your control to theirs. Email accounts can also be valuable to hackers because they provide valuable information about you, and the account itself can be used to spread spam and malware to your contacts.

Unless you are using additional tools to prevent fraud, which will be discussed later, all a hacker needs to take over an online account is your username and password. These two things are called your "credentials." Websites for which you are registered will check your credentials before you can get access to your account. If a hacker obtains your credentials, they will have the ability to access your online account with those credentials and start their dirty work.

In this chapter, we will look at bank account takeovers. The three most common ways that a hacker can obtain your bank login credentials are as follows:

Malware installed on your computer.

The topic of malware was discussed in a previous chapter. (Remember, the word "malware" is derived from "malicious" and "software".) One type of malware can obtain your keystrokes as you type them on your keyboard. This malware contains commands which send your keystrokes to hackers. Once this happens, they may be able to use them to log in to your accounts.

So, let's say you clicked on an attachment in a phishing email by mistake and downloaded keystroke logging malware onto your computer. When you use the computer to log in to your bank account by typing your username and password, the malware will send that information to the hackers. Many types of malware that are used to do this will also be able to show the hackers the website that you are visiting when you log in. If they know the website and your login credentials, they will then try to log in to your online bank account.

In many cases, banks have defenses that will prevent this from happening without additional information from the hackers. For example, if the hackers try to log in to your bank account from a computer that the bank doesn't recognize because you have not used that computer to log in before, it might ask the hacker to answer "challenge questions," such as your place of birth or the city where you got married. However, if controls like this are not in place, or if the hacker has done their homework and knows enough about you through your public social media postings, they might still be able to gain access to your online bank account.

Your best defense against keylogging malware, as discussed earlier, is to be careful where you click and not to download anything from unknown senders.

Also, keep a close eye on your financial accounts. Check your balances often and have the bank send you an email or text message whenever money is taken out of your bank account.

If you see anything unusual or suspect fraud with your bank account, contact your bank right away. Consumer protection laws generally protect your money against fraud if the fraud is reported within 60 days of its occurrence.

They ask you for it.

A second way that hackers may obtain your login credentials is to simply ask you for them. This trick involves a phishing email that is designed to look like the sender is your bank. Here is an example of how the scheme might work, beginning with the original fake bank email:

From: yourbank@alerts.com
To: youremail@email.com
Subject: Fraud Alert! Suspicious activity in your account.

Your bank would like to verify some recent activity on your account.
To protect you from unauthorized access we have restricted your online access which remain in effect.
To safeguard your account, require that you confirm your banking details.
Help speed up this process please access the following link so we can complete the verification.

In the above email, notice that the bank's logo and slogan are pasted into the email to make it look more realistic. (I'm using a generic bank name to protect the identities of the banks that have been affected by this scam. This example is based on a real case involving a real bank, but it could be any bank, including yours.)

I have underlined the words the hackers have used to elicit an emotional reaction. Remember, it is much easier to trick victims into making bad decisions when the victim is in an emotional state.

Circled is the link the hackers want the victim to click. In this example, the click leads to a web page set up by the hackers to steal personal information. Here is what that page looks like:

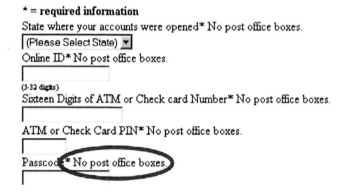

Illustration 1 of 3

Logic and common sense would tell us that this is a scam just from looking at the words circled, because they don't make sense in this context. But remember, a victim may not be using common sense at this point because their emotions have been fired up by the email.

Illustration 2 of 3

The fill-in form continues in Illustration 2. At the bottom of this page, the hackers, acting like they are your bank, ask for the account number and routing number for your bank account. Wouldn't your bank already have that information?

Contact Information

* = required information
Phone Number* First 3 digits of Phone Number
Second 3 digits of Phone Number   - Last 4 digits of Phone Number
E-mail Address*

E-mail Password*

Identification Information

* = required information
Social Security Number*
First 3 digits of Social Security Number   - Second 2 Digits of Social Security Number   - Last 4 digits of Social
Security Number   Why do we ask for this?
Date of Birth*
        Day
Month2-digit2-digit
month of   day of Year 4-digit year of birth
birth   birth

(format: mm-dd-yyyy)
Mother Maiden Name*

Mother Middles Name*

Father Maiden Name*

Father Middles Name

Illustration 3 of 3

In Illustration 3, notice in the first box the blank spaces for your email address and password. Why would your bank need the password to your email account?

In the second box is the request for your social security number. That number, as you learned earlier, is the key to stealing your identity outright.

In the third box there is a request for your "mother maiden name." Sometimes this is provided as a security feature on legitimate accounts. Notice, however, that right underneath that is a request for "father maiden name." If a victim has not figured out this is a scam by now, this should do it. As we all know, it should say "father's maiden name." You need the possessive form of the word—we learned that in elementary school! On a serious note, though, there aremany mistakes in this form, including gramma, that should alert you that it is a fraud.

But even aside from that, as a rule you should simply never provide personal information in response to an unsolicited request. If you adhere to this tenet, your online account cannot be taken over through this technique.

They send you to a fake website.

A third common way that hackers can take over our bank accounts is by website spoofing. In this scenario, the victim receives a phishing email designed to look like it is coming from the victim's bank. The email requests that the victim click on a website link contained in the email. The link, if clicked, will direct the victim's computer to a fake bank website with a place for the victim to enter their login credentials.

The illustration below is based on a real example and shows how the scam works.

Your Bank
Grow Your Money With Us

Dear customer!
As you know, your bank always cares first of all for comfort and safety of the users. To make our service even more convenient and to improve results of mutual partnership we have made a decision to specify some features by asking our users.
The most convenient way is, certainly, to do it online. We suggest you to go to the link:

https://www.yourbank.8647.bizweb/customers/survey

and to answer some questions. We respect and we appreciate you and your free time, therefore we offer you for some minutes, required for filling in the questioning, compensation in amount of $15 that will be sent to your personal account.

Again, "Your Bank" is a fictitious name, as I don't think the actual bank in this example would want their name used here. Individuals receiving the above email who don't bank at "Your Bank" will likely disregard it. Additionally, many people who are customers of the bank will recognize the email as a fake and disregard it. But that is where the concept of phishing works its magic for scammers, as the law of large numbers applies itself. Thousands, if not millions of copies of this email have been sent. There are likely to be numerous people who receive the email, are customers of the bank, don't recognize that it is fake, and click on the link embedded in the email.

In this version of a phishing email, the scam or trick is in the link.

Your Bank
Grow Your Money With Us

Dear customer!
As you know, your bank always cares first of all for comfort and safety of the users. To make our service even more convenient and to improve results of mutual partnership we have made a decision to specify some features by asking our users.
The most convenient way is, certainly, to do it online.
We suggest you to go to the link:

The trick
is in  https://www.yourbank.8647.bizweb/customers/survey
the link

We respect and we appreciate you and your free time, therefore we offer you for some minutes, required for filling in the questioning, compensation in amount of $15 that will be sent to your personal account.

The motivation to click on the link comes from the emotional enticement in the email. That is, the email recipient will be paid $15 for "filling in the questioning." How do you get to the place to do this? Click on the link. Emotions are again an important component in this example, because subjugating logic and common sense to emotion will cause you to overlook the poor grammar, which on its own is an indication of fraud.

What's the actual trick here? What happens when you click the link?

The trick here is to steal the victim's login credentials for their online bank account. When the link is clicked by the unsuspecting victim it will bring them to a website that looks very much like the real bank website, but it is not. It is a website that the scammers have created to mimic the real thing, complete with blank boxes for the user's login credentials.

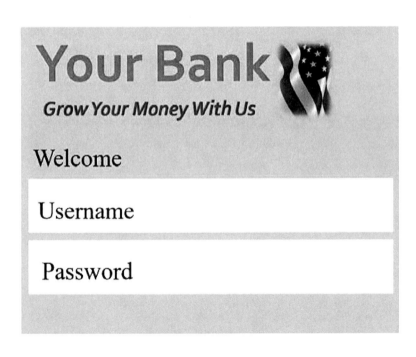

Since the website is controlled by the scammers, a username and password that is typed into the boxes will go right to them.

To give the scammers time to withdraw money from the victim's bank account, they need to make sure that the victim does not try to log themselves in at the legitimate site, as this may prevent the scammers from doing so. The scammers might cause a message to appear on the victim's computer to achieve this, as in the example seen below.

We sincerely apologize for the inconvenience. Our site is currently undergoing scheduled maintenance and upgrades, but will return shortly. Thank you for your patience.

Most banks have gotten much better at preventing this type of fraud. In this example, the scammers might still be denied access to a bank account, even with the proper login credentials, unless they go through additional hoops, like answering a challenge question. But in many cases the scheme has worked for the scammers, and money has been withdrawn from breached bank accounts.

Bank account takeover summary

We have looked at the three most common ways that hackers can obtain our login credentials for our bank accounts. In each of these examples, the hackers have created an emotional hook to trick their victims. For this reason, it is important to remember to never let your emotions overcome logic and common sense. Additionally, never provide personal information in response to an unsolicited email.

Despite this type of fraud, don't be reluctant to use online banking. Generally, if you do become a victim of a computer scam as described in this chapter, your money is protected and will be reimbursed to you by the bank if you report the fraud within 60 days. But we certainly don't want to wait that long. We don't want the hackers getting any of our money to begin with. If the profit incentive is lowered or eliminated, then maybe at some point it will help to mitigate or eliminate the problem of bank account takeovers.

Chapter 8
Email Account Hijacking

There are 2.4 million emails sent every second; 74 trillion emails every year.

Radicati Group

Have you ever received an email that looked like this?

From: Johnny Bones

To: You

Johnny Bones has invited you to view the
following document:

Open in Docs

Illustration 1 – A trick to hijack your email account

    If so, were you curious about the document? Did you click on "Open in Docs?" If you did, the next thing you may have seen on your computer was this:

Sign in with your email account

Email

Password

Next

Illustration 2 – Login page to steal your email account credentials

If you filled in the boxes with your email address (username) and password, you may have provided those credentials to hackers. The hackers will use those credentials to log in to your email and create all sorts of havoc.

So what types of havoc can hackers cause with access to an email account? Plenty. I'll get to that. But first, it is important to know that the above illustrations show the method by which hackers can "hijack" your email account. Hijacking, in this context, means "stealing" or "taking over."

Illustration 1 shows the phishing email, which was probably sent to millions of email addresses. Many of the recipients may not even be users of that email service, but many will, since the usual targets are free email services like AOL, Gmail, and Yahoo.

A person receiving this email may be tempted to click "Open in Docs" to see what document is awaiting them.

Illustration 2 shows the fake login page for the targeted email account. To see the document, you must fill in your email address and the password to your email account.

In reality, there is no actual document to be seen. The whole thing is a trick to get you to give your email credentials to the hackers, and they will get them if you fill in the boxes labeled "email" and "password." Your email will then have been hijacked.

Dear Mail User,

Your mailbox has exceeded it storage limit as set by your
administrator and you will not be able to send and receive new
mails until you re-validate it click on validate below to do so.

Validate

Change will take effect immediately.

Sincerely,

Admin.

Illustration 3 – Another attempt to direct you to a fake login page.

Illustration 3 shows how hackers, again, are trying to elicit an emotional reaction from the person who receives this email. A person who believes they will no longer be able to receive email might click on "validate," which will direct their browser to a fake login page that looks like the one in illustration 2.

Let's get back to the havoc the hackers can create with access to your email account and its list of contacts. For the sake of simplicity, let's use the term "friend" to describe your contacts (who could be friends, relatives, or other people). Here are the most common nefarious things that hackers can do once they have hijacked your email account.

Send spam your friends

Hackers will use your email account to spread links for advertisements. A person is more likely to click on a link if they think it is coming from you, rather than a stranger. If your friend clicks on the links, they will be sent to a website that is marketing products through real or bogus claims. Even if your friend doesn't buy anything, they might provide click revenue for the person who sent the spam. A typical ad might be for low-priced pharmaceuticals from Canada.

Send malware to your contacts

The topic of malware was discussed in a previous chapter. One of the ways that malware is spread is through email account hijacking. Once the hacker has control of your email account, they can send emails containing attachments or links to all your friends. Again, the hacker is taking advantage of your relationships with your contacts to get them to click. The click can cause malware to download or send your friend to a website that could infect their computer.

If you receive an email from a friend whose email account has been hijacked, it might look something like this:

From: Your friend

To: You

Subject: You gotta see this!

http://www.uinud86.ohk.com

Illustration 4 – Beware of emails that only contain a link, even if the email looks like it is from someone you know.

Notice that all you see in the email is the link. This is a telltale sign that your friend's email account has been hijacked because most people would not send an email with just a link. It you want to avoid malware and spam-related websites, it is important not to click on these links. Your best course of action is to mark this email as spam, which should cause your email provider to send the email to a spam folder. In the future, your email provider will begin to recognize these emails and send them automatically to the spam folder. Note that emails like this may originate from different email addresses, so your spam filter may not catch them each time. It is also a good idea to empty the spam folder often, which reduces the risk that you will be affected by these emails.

Ask your friends for money

There are several types of scams that fall under this category. One involves the hackers sending messages from the victim's email account to their list of friends. The messages might say that the victim (the email account owner whose account was hijacked) is in trouble. One common scam looks like the one below.

> I'm sorry for this odd request because it might get to you too urgent but it's because of the situation of things right now, I'm stuck London, United Kingdom with family right now, we came down here on vacation, we were robbed, worse of it was that our bags, cash, credit cards and cell phone were stolen from us at GUN POINT, it's such a crazy experience for us, we need help flying back home, we still have some money in our account but we don't have access to it right here. the authorities are not being 100% supportive to the matter but the good thing is that we still have our passports but don't have enough money to clear the hotel bills, please I need you to loan me $2,250 USD, I'll reimburse you as soon as I'm back home. PROMISE, you have my word, hope to read from you soon.

This example illustrates the use of emotion to trick people. A friend is in trouble in a foreign country and they need help. An emotional reaction might lead one to respond to the email and do as instructed. A logical reaction, however, would be to contact the person who is supposedly in trouble by phone to verify that they need help.

Ask your bank for money

When a hacker has control of your email account they can scan through past emails, including those that you sent, those that you received, and even those that you deleted if your email "trash" has not been emptied. You can imagine how much a hacker can learn about people from their emails. They will know who your friends are, where you shop, what you do for hobbies, what groups you belong to, and, most importantly for hackers, where you conduct your financial transactions (that includes banks, financial advisors, credit card companies, mortgage companies, etc.)

Hackers tend to hone in on financial accounts because, to put it very simply, that's where the money is. For starters, they will send you targeted phishing emails that are customized to look like they come from your bank. Even more common, the hackers will send an email message from your email account to your financial institutions. The email message will invariably be for a wire transfer request from your bank account to the hackers. Most financial institutions have strict protocols about wiring money based on an email request. Part of the protocols include talking to the account holder before a wire is sent to confirm the legitimacy of the request. But this doesn't always happen the way that it should. There have been many examples where banks and financial advisors let their guard down or were tricked by the hackers to a degree where they didn't think they needed to call to verify.

For example, one person—we'll call him Mike to protect his identity—told me an interesting story after he heard me present on the topic of cybercrime. He said that his email was hijacked, most likely through one of the tricks previously described. The hacker learned where Mike banked by looking at his past emails. The hacker also learned something somewhat peculiar about the way Mike composed his emails—they were in all capital letters. Mike told me that he didn't like to shift between upper and lower case on the keyboard, so he just typed everything in upper case. Mike's numerous communications to his personal banker were composed only of upper-case letters.

The hacker must have paid special attention to this, because when the hacker composed the email to Mike's personal banker requesting a wire transfer, he did it in all caps.

Mike told me that his banker received the email requesting the wire transfer and sent the money to the hacker's bank account without calling Mike first. The total amount was $8,000.

When Mike discovered the wire transfer, he contacted his banker. The banker explained that he sent the money without checking with Mike because the email was in capital letters. The banker must have thought that only his customer, Mike, would write emails that way, so it must have come from him. So out went the money.

Hackers that hijack email accounts to commit wire transfer fraud know that they must trick the financial institution into believing the email is really from the victim. If there is any question, they will call to verify, which they should do in any case.

So, who is hit with the loss in this case? The answer is the bank. Mike was not responsible for loss, even though his email account was hijacked. That part was his fault. But because the banker should have called Mike to verify the wire transfer request, the bank put the $8,000 back into Mike's bank account at their expense.

This fraud could have easily been prevented if the banker had called Mike to verify the wire transfer. But is that the only way it could have been prevented? No, the hacker would not have had access to Mike's email account in the first place if it had not been hijacked. The hijacking was Mike's fault and it could have been prevented if Mike had been more careful about logging into his email account.

Another example comes from a financial advisor named Paul, who was in an audience to which I was presenting. I was talking about email account hijacking during the presentation when Paul threw his hand up in the air.

Hello Paul,

I was involve in an accident yesterday and right now I am in the hospital and doctor said I cant make use of the phone for now or go out of the hospital due to my health condition, I am having problem transferring money online from my account to my sister account can you please have this complete for me and what is the information you need from her account to have it done,

Thanks.

An email received from the client of a financial advisor whose email account had been hijacked.

"Hey, look at this," he said.

Paul had glanced down at his phone during my presentation and saw an email to him from one of his clients.

"I just got one of those!" he yelled out. "What's that?" I said.

"An email asking for a wire transfer from a client's email account," he replied.

It was almost as though the situation had been arranged by me and Paul for dramatic effect while I was talking about the very topic of email account hijacking. It was actually just a coincidence, but a good one, as it made a crucial point about how common these transfer scams are.

Paul didn't fall for this scam, but, unfortunately, many have, and hackers continue to profit from a crime that is almost always preventable.

Real Estate Wire Transfer Fraud

If I told that a crime that was associated with $ 19 million dollars in fraud in one calendar year and $ 969 million the next year, you might conclude that the trend for this crime is steep. That is exactly how the FBI describes real estate wire transfer fraud.

This crime starts with an email account hijacking. The email account could belong to a potential home buyer, but more likely it belongs to a real estate company, title company or an attorney that is involved in home sale and purchase transactions.

Once criminals have access to the email account of the target, they will search for pending home purchase closings. Just before a closing is scheduled to occur, the criminal will send an email to the home buyer from the hijacked email account. This email will request that the home buyer wire transfer closing funds and contain instructions on where to send the money. If these instructions are followed by the home buyer, the money for the closing ends up in the criminal's bank account.

There have large losses across the country from the scheme. Home buyers are usually the ones who absorb the loss if the money can't be recovered.

The scheme I just described is a symptom of the problem that results from the real problem of people and business getting their email accounts hijacked. The best prevention is to not fall for the tricks exemplified in this chapter that are used to hijack email accounts and never log in to an email account through a link.

Regarding wire transfers for home purchase or any reason, it is critical that you never wire transfer money based on email instructions alone. Always talk to the recipient to verify wire transfer instructions.

Chapter Summary

Email account hijacking is a very common type of cybercrime that is easy to commit. With this crime, the ultimate goal of the hacker is to make money directly by requesting cash from a person or a financial institution. They can also make money indirectly by sending you to websites that sell fake or overpriced products or by spreading malware across the internet.

The conduit for this activity is a victim's email account. To stay safe, always log in to your email account through your internet service provider's home page or directly on the website of the email provider. Don't click on links to log in, and don't click on emails sent to you that contain only a link. Finally, if you are asked via email to send money to a friend in need, always verify the legitimacy of the request by contacting the friend or the friend's family by phone.

Jeff Lanza

Chapter 9
Passwords and Passphrases

"To help remember it, I used my dog's name as my computer password. Then I heard you need to have a strong password, so I changed my dogs name to 8#ApnSrQ."

Unknown

What are your favorite passwords? Are any of yours on this list of the most common computer passwords used in the United States in 2018:

123456	password
12345678	1234
qwerty	1q2w3e
1234	football
12345	baseball
Welcome	abc123
1111	dragon
Master	google
letmein	login
princess	qwertyuiop

I believe most people hate passwords. Here is a partial list of issues that make us hate passwords:

- You are not supposed to write them down, but you can't remember them.

- You don't want to store them on a computer, because the computer might get hacked and the criminals will have all your passwords.
- You don't want to let a third party store your passwords because the third party might get hacked and the criminals will have all your passwords.
- You find it difficult to come up with a password that meets the requirements of the online account that you are trying to set up.
- When you do come up with a password that meets the requirements of the online account that you've set up, the site, after what seems like very little time, asks that you change the password.
- The site continues to ask you to change your password, even if you like the one you have and don't want to.
- If you put in the wrong password a few times on a website, it locks you out and sends a reset password to your email account.
- You try to log in to your email account to get the reset password, but you can't remember the password to your email account.
- In addition to entering a password which you can't remember, the website wants to send a code to your phone to enter in the website after you enter a password which you can't remember.

Any of these things sound familiar?

Unfortunately, it seems like we are stuck with passwords until biometric logins become more reliable or until someone comes up with a better way to limit account access to only those who should have that access (in other words, a way that allows you to get in, but keeps criminals out).

In this chapter, we will discuss some ways to deal with passwords that won't give you fits.

Strong Passwords

You have probably heard the term "strong password," maybe more than once, or more than a hundred times. The term seems to get mentioned quite a bit during conversations about computer security. There is good news on that front! The definition of a strong password has changed and the change is going to make it easier for us to deal with passwords. We will get to all of that shortly.

A password needs to be strong to protect access to the online account from computer programs that use brute force, or the power of computers, to keep guessing passwords until they have obtained access.

Most online accounts will forbid access if the wrong password is used more than three times. One might think that if this is the case, a weak password will suffice, as it is unlikely that a brute force attack will have success within three tries. This is true, and weak passwords would probably be fine, except for one thing, which has to do with the way user passwords are stored on sites they will be used to access. To protect them on the sites from hackers, the passwords are assigned a "hash value," which is used to disguise the password. The hackers have to know the hash value to obtain stored passwords if they hack into a website. In some cases, they can learn the hash value by hacking into the website through a separate mechanism aside from the brute force program, perhaps through a flaw on the site.

If the passwords are weak, the associated hash value will be weak as well, and the hackers might be able to guess it. Then, once they have the hash value, they can use brute force to guess the passwords on another computer. Once guessed, they can apply it to the website they are trying to access.

This is all a roundabout way to say that strong passwords are a necessity to protect online accounts. So why don't all people use strong passwords? And why don't websites require their usage? If you think that most people are using strong passwords, think again. The security firm Keeper analyzed over 10 million passwords that were made public through hacks. It found that about half of the passwords were composed of the ones listed in the beginning of this chapter.

Do you use any passwords on this list? If so, you should change them to strong passwords for better security.

Notice a couple of popular passwords, "qwerty," and "qwertyuiop." Aren't they nice? You don't have to remember them, and you don't have to write them down, because they are already written down on the keyboard itself.

If you are using any of the above passwords, or other keyboard character sequences as passwords, you should discontinue this practice! Let's not make it easy for hackers—they are aware of the common password list.

So how do you make it more difficult for the hackers to gain access to your online accounts? Use strong passwords.

You might ask, "What is a strong password?"

That is a great question because the answer to it changed in June 2017. That's when the National Institute of Standards and Technology (NIST) announced new password guidelines. Out with the old, in with the new.

Here are the old and new strong password guidelines:

Old Guidelines:

- Minimum of eight characters in length
- Containing upper and lowercase
- Containing numbers
- Containing keyboard symbols

New Guidelines:

- Minimum of eight characters in length

Weird, isn't it? For all these years we have been told to use complicated passwords like $AQuR83X. And now they tell us they are not necessary. In fact, a long password without all the complexity is more secure. Wow!

There is a caveat, however. The new guidelines specify that the password must exclude some things.

So here is what not to use in your eight-character or longer password:

1. commonly-used, expected or compromised passwords or from previous breaches, such as: the twenty words listed in the first part of this chapter and words like those (some are the less than eight characters anyway)
2. dictionary words and repetitive or sequential characters such as "aaaaaaa"
3. 1234abcd
4. The name of a service such as Yahoo
5. A username such as "Johnsmith"
6. Derivatives of usernames such as "Johnsmith7890"

Passphrases

Instead of using the term *passwords,* let's call them *passphrases*. Passphrases, are words you might use in a sentence, combined as one long word. An example:

paranoiawillnotdestroyya

A little paranoia is good when it comes up to passphrase length. The longer, the better. Even though the above passphrase does not have added complexity of numbers and symbols, it is strong because of the length. The longer it is, the stronger it is. If you want to mix it up, you can still add numbers and symbols to your heart's content.

Many of your online accounts may still require the more complex passphrase containing upper and lower case, a number and a symbol. Even though the new guidelines have been announced, we may still need to use passphrases based on the old guidelines for some websites.

Changing Passphrases on a Regular Basis

Another newsflash: it is not necessary to routinely change your passphrases. If have a strong passphrase, you don't necessarily need to change it unless someone has obtained it that you don't trust or if the account it protects has been breached.

Unique Passphrases

If you use the same passphrase for multiple accounts, you are exposed to additional hacks across all the accounts that utilize the same passphrase, if one is breached. One example of this risk is represented by a case where a popular restaurant chain's computer was hacked, providing the criminals with usernames and passwords of registered users of the restaurant site. Those same credentials were then used online to attempt to gain access to other online sites. Where the passwords were the same, the criminals purchased hundreds of thousands of dollars of goods. This fraud would have been easily prevented if the users of the sites utilized different passwords for each site.

For maximum security, you should have a unique strong passphrase for each of your accounts. For some, that may mean having fifty or more unique passphrases. Managing this number of unique passphrases to be difficult. Clicking on "forgot password", can be very frustrating and time-consuming process of resetting your passphrase. In some cases, it may involve calling a support number, which is always a barrel of fun. This process can be avoided only if you remember to do one thing: remember your passphrase! This is unlikely if you have a lot of passphrases. Here's the next best option: manage your passphrases in a way in which they will always be at your disposal without counting on your memory. If you do not already have a secure system to manage your passphrases, consider the following ideas.

Passphrase Management

1. **Write them down.** This old-fashioned tried-and-true method works well if you are accessing online

accounts from a computer in your home, because a written page of passphrases is not something you want to carry around with you. Now, I know that some of you are saying, "Wait a minute! I thought it was a bad idea to write down passphrases." It is a bad practice to write down passphrases in the way that most people do, that is, on a sticky tab stuck on the computer keyboard. Here is a better option: write down your passphrases on a piece of paper and lock the paper in a drawer or file, to be removed only when you need it. If that locked place is accessed by anyone other than you or someone you trust, then you should immediately change your passphrases. Even better, you can make the written passphrases slightly different than the actual passphrases. For example, say your actual passphrase is:

thepigjumpedoverthemoon

Instead of writing that passphrase on the piece of paper, you might write:

thepigjumpeDoverthemoon

You have just changed one letter. We will call it your personal low-tech encryption program! Use any method you would like to disguise the written passphrase but keep it simple and easy to remember. If someone finds the piece of paper with your passphrases, it will be useless to them without your personal encryption key. If you want to use Microsoft's word-processing program, Word, you can encrypt the document in a high-tech way. Use the "save as" feature in Word and click on the box labeled "Protect

Document." You will be asked for a passphrase, which, once entered, will be required to open the document. This feature also encrypts the document on your computer, a further way to keep its contents secure. Nobody will be able to view the document with the passphrase (and that includes you, so don't forget the passphrase to the document, because Microsoft has no way to recover your passphrase).

2. **Use a smartphone to store passphrases.** I'm not referring to putting your passphrases in contact information on your smartphone. One reason that's not secure is because you may grant some smartphone apps access to your contacts, hence giving the apps access to your passphrases. A better option is to use the "notes" app on a smartphone to store your passphrases. You can secure the "notes" app when you save it, so that it can only be opened with another passphrase or PIN.

3. **Use a passphrase management program.** A very popular and secure option for storing passphrases is a passphrase manager. This is a software program that will create and store passphrases on your computer, the cloud, a separate device, or all of these. Most passphrase managers can sync all your passphrases across various devices, such as computers, phones, and tablets. Popular brands include Dashlane, LastPass, Keeper, KeePass, 1Password, and KeyChain for Apple products. There are both free versions and paid versions of these products, and it is mostly a matter of personal preference as to which product would work best for you. For most of them, you can test the product with a trial before having to commit any money. The most important question that people ask me about passphrase managers is about security. In general,

passphrase managers are very secure and are an excellent choice for dealing with passphrases. It is important when considering a passphrase manager that you read the company's website, especially as pertains to security. The program is most secure when the employees can't see your passphrases and the passphrases are encrypted.

4. **Browser storage of passphrases.** I am often asked if it is okay to let computer browsers, such as Internet Explorer, Firefox, and Chrome, store passphrases. This is generally not recommended, because the passphrases might be accessible to and useable by three different parties. The first are cyber criminals who may have hacked into your computer. Second are people who have stolen your computer or have found it if you happen to lose it. Third are others who may have legitimate access to your computer, but whom you might not want prying around on your bank site, like friends, roommates, or a weird cousin.

Chapter Summary

The use of strong passphrases is imperative to maintain online security. A strong passphrase has at least eight characters without using dictionary words, common passphrases, usernames or service names or derivatives of such, should use a unique strong passphrase for each of your online accounts, but as an absolute minimum you should have at least ten unique passphrases for the ten distinct categories of your online accounts. There are many ways to store and retrieve your passphrases in a secure fashion, and the way you choose to do so is a function of your lifestyle, how much effort you want to invest, and whether you want to spend a few bucks on a passphrase manager.

For even better login security, use 2FA. You might ask, "What's 2FA?". Read on, my friend, read on.

Chapter 10
Two-Factor Authentication

If you have used an ATM card or debit card, you have used two-factor authentication.

The Federal Trade Commission (FTC) recently conducted a test by posting fake information about consumers to websites that hackers use to trade in stolen credentials. Within minutes, the crooks used the information to try to access the fake email, payment, and credit card accounts.

In real life, we have no control over how our information is protected by third parties. If a breach occurs and our information shows up on hacker trading sites, crooks will pounce quickly, as indicated by this test. If the information had been that of real people, they would have become victims of account hijacking and takeovers.

Given this risk, it is important to understand a very effective method of protecting your accounts. It is called two-factor authentication.

The concept of two-factor authentication may seem unfamiliar to some, but it really shouldn't, because most of us use it every day in one form or another. Using a key to unlock the front door of your house is an example of two- factor authentication. If you don't have the key, you can't get in the house. But you also need to know where the house is located. If you have the key and don't know where the house is, you still won't be able to get in.

Two-factor authentication means that to "authenticate" yourself as an authorized person who is allowed to enter an area, you must be able to provide two things. These two things are generally something you have and something you know. In the case of a house, you have a key and you know the location of the house

Most hotels use two-factor authentication for room access, which provides greater security than one factor. A magnetic key card used to access a hotel room is useless unless you know the room number. Similarly, if you know the room number but don't have the magnetic card, you can't get in the room. So, you need both things, or two factors.

Something you know

Something you have

The room number is something you know and the key card is something you have. In the old days, hotels didn't have magnetic cards, just keys with room numbers engraved on them. If hotel guest lost the key and it was found by someone else, that person had both factors and they could get into the room. This was not a very secure system.

If you use an ATM card or a debit card, you have used two-factor authentication. The card is something you have; the PIN number is something you know.

Two-Factor Authentication For Computer Access

The concept of two-factor authentication works the same way when applied to computers. You know your username and password and you have something else. Usually what you have is a code that is sent by text message to your phone. To enter the online site, you need to enter both: what you know (username and password) and what you have (the code sent to you). The thing that you have could also be something physical, like a thumb drive.

Two-factor authentication may sometimes be referred to by other terms. If you see these terms, they mean the same two-step process to protect your accounts which we have been discussing: *Two-step authentication; Two-factor verification; Two-step verification; 2FA.*

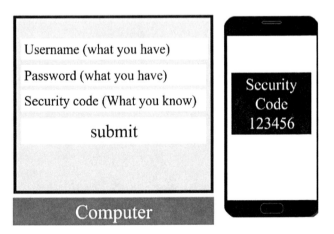

Let's call it 2FA from now on. 2FA is a fantastic way to add extra security to your account login. To make you a victim of a breach, a hacker would have to have your username and password and the security code which has been sent to your phone. It's not impossible for them to have both factors, but it's highly unlikely, since they would need access to your phone. The use of 2FA is highly recommended because it can prevent most cases of email account hijacking and bank account takeovers.

How to Implement Two-Factor Authentication

Many financial websites automatically employ 2FA if they don't recognize a computer or Internet Protocol (IP) address that is being used to log in to their sites. So, you may already have had experience with this procedure. In addition, sites like Google, Facebook, Yahoo, LinkedIn, and others offer 2FA, but you must opt in. The opt-in process is generally found in the "settings" section of the various sites.

It's Not as Inconvenient as You Think

Most computer users don't like to have to go through too many steps to do anything. It's too inconvenient, they say. While it's true that using 2FA is less convenient than not using it, it is much more secure. But here's the deal: you don't have to use 2FA every time you log in. You can set it up that way if you want, and I know people who do because they want maximum security. But if you want both convenience and extra security, you can set up 2FA to engage only if the site doesn't recognize the computer that's being used to log in. In other words, you won't have to use 2FA every time. You'll only have to use it the first time, or any time you are using a different computer or IP address to log in than what you have used previously. So, most of the time, you will not be taking the extra step (but Google, for example, will ask you to take the extra step every 30 days, even if you are using the same computer as before. Just trying to keep it honest!)

Now pay attention to this part, because it's the part that will thwart the hackers and keep you safe.

Let's say that a hacker obtains your username and password through a computer breach, a fake login trick that fooled you (discussed earlier), or another way.

The hacker will try to use your stolen credentials to log in to your account, but they don't have your phone, so they can't obtain the "something you know" part of the log in process. Wala! We have stopped the hacker dead in their tracks.

2FA is a very effective way to keep your accounts secure. Most financial websites use it as a default. But for your other accounts, employ it where available, especially for email and social media websites.

Logging-in through social media accounts

For some it can be very frustrating to engage in online commerce because on some websites, you must create an online account to make a purchase or view a page. You may not prefer not to set up another online account, with another username and password to deal with. If you are in this camp, there is another option, but only if the site allows you to use it. That option is to log in with your Google account or a social media account such as Facebook.

Let's say for instance, that you are trying to order some flowers on the site called "Flowers by Irene," or "FBI" for short. You don't want to set up a username and passwords for this site, but FBI requires it for you to order the flowers.

FBI might give you the option (this is very common on commerce sites) to log in with your Google account. Assuming you have a Google account, you can use it to log in to the FBI site.

This is a convenient way to log in and here is the good part: you are not providing your Google credentials to FBI. Google is just verifying you to FBI. This will allow you, in this example, to order the flowers without signing up for an FBI account. By the way, if you have engaged 2FA for your Google account, the whole process has become even more secure.

Chapter Summary

Two-factor authentication is a great way to secure your online accounts. You should use it for all your important and sensitive accounts, including your email and financial accounts. It is easy to setup and not as inconvenient as you might think to use because the PIN is not needed for every login.

Jeff Lanza

Chapter 11
Wi-Fi Security

Imagine asking a barista at coffee shop this question: "What's the password for your IEEE 802.11b Direct Sequence?"

If you had devised a technology that you wanted to market on a mass scale to generate wide acceptance, would you call it "IEEE 802.11b Direct Sequence?"

How about something a little catchier? Maybe, "Wi-Fi?"

The term "Wi-Fi" was devised by a brand consulting firm and has been in use since about 1999. The term may have been a play on an older term, "hi-fi," which was a shortened version of a term used to describe sound, "high fidelity." The "wi" is short for wireless, but the "fi" in Wi-Fi does not stand for fidelity, or anything else for that matter.

Wi-Fi refers to a wireless network that uses radio waves to provide internet or network connections. You will find Wi-Fi almost everywhere that you go, and in your home too if you opt for this service.

Wi-Fi at home

If you have wireless internet at your home, then you are familiar with the convenience of being "unplugged" (as opposed to being "unglued" when the wireless internet doesn't work like it's supposed to). The wireless was so bad at my house a few years ago that my wife subjected herself to the agonizing pain of a call to the customer service department of our internet service provider (ISP). In general, our ISP has done an excellent job of taking "serve" out of the word "service." If you do that, you're not left with much of a word, or much service.

Our internet speeds were dreadfully slow, and my wife (MW) complained to the customer care representative (CCR) who was a big obnoxious jerk. He acted like it was our problem that their internet was slow. At one point the conversation between the (CCR) and MW went like this:

MW: Our internet speed is very slow.

CCR: Are you going to cancel our service?

MW: No.

CCR: Then I can't help you.

MW: We just want the internet speeds that you promise in your ads.

CCR: The ad says, "up to." You know what that means?

MW: I know what "up to" means, but we are not getting anything close to that and the internet keeps cutting out too. Is there anything you can do?

CCR: Actually, I can boost your speed from here. Stand by and I will do it for you.

CCR: (10 minutes later) Okie dokie, you're all set. I boosted your speed.

By this time, MW knew something was up, so she called back and talked to another so called CCR, who told her that there was no way they could boost speed from their location. Shortly after, we got a new ISP. So far MW has not had to talk to any more CCRs, which is a good thing, if you like to remain sane.

As it pertains to security, the wonderful thing about a home Wi-Fi network is that you are in control of the security. Here are a few important things to do to make sure your home Wi-Fi network is secure, whether it is you that is setting it up or someone else.

Name your network

Give the network that you are going to use a name, so it is easy to find. You can name it anything that you want. I might name my network "Jeff's home network." It is fine to create a name like this but know that your neighbors will be able to see that you have a network by this name. However, they won't be able to access it unless they have your password.

Create a strong password for your network

This is very important because it will ensure that anyone other than your authorized users (who know the password) will not be able to use your network. If a bad actor (a term the FBI likes to use to describe crooks, hackers, and spies) were to get into to your Wi-Fi network, anything they do online would appear as though it were coming from your Internet Protocol (IP) address. If it is criminal activity, you might be accused of their crimes. I'm not making this up, this has happened!

So, use the protocol discussed earlier when creating a strong password, that is, create a password of at least eight characters with the exclusions mentioned in Chapter 9. When you set up the password, keep in mind that the software prompts and documentation may refer to the password as an "encryption key" or "pass-key." These terms also refer to the password.

Create a guest account for visitors

If you plan on allowing guests in your home to use your Wi-Fi network, set up a separate network on your router for guests. Create a strong password for this network, but don't use the same password as your home network. After your guest departs, you can change the password for the guest network to restrict any further access and keep the same password for your regular network.

Encrypt your network

Encrypting your network secures the communication from point to point. For example, the words you type in an email on your laptop are encrypted before they travel from your laptop to the Wi-Fi router.

There are three common encryption standards for Wi-Fi networks, referred to as WPA2, WPA, and WEP. Of the three, WPA2 is the most secure and should be the one that you use if you have a choice.

Public Wi-Fi hotspots

Public Wi-Fi networks, often referred to as "Wi-Fi hotspots," have become a ubiquitous offering in retail establishments and other places we visit. Most coffee shops, pubs, restaurants, bars, airports, hotels, etc., have a Wi-Fi network that has been set up for public use. Sometimes these networks require a password, but in other cases, you can access the network without one.

There are security concerns that you should be aware of when accessing public Wi-Fi networks. Mainly, these networks are not secure. With a little expertise, a person can see who is connected to the network and what they are doing on it. They might even trick you by setting up a lookalike network that people may connect to instead of the merchant's actual network.

Security cannot be guaranteed with public Wi-Fi hotspots, so here are two options that may help you be more secure.

A Virtual Private Network

You can have security in public hotspots by using a virtual private network (VPN). You need special software on your computer to use a VPN. There are many choices here. Most VPN software costs about $3-5 per month. The VPN software will create a secure tunnel between your computer and the websites that you are accessing, which will prevent eavesdropping.

Mobile Hotspot

Another secure way to access websites securely in a public area is to use your smartphone as a hotspot. Most newer model smartphones have this capability. You can connect to it by turning the hotspot on in your settings and then finding and connecting to that network on your computer. If you do that, you will be using the cellular network of your phone for internet access. This is generally more secure than the Wi-Fi hotspot. It may be slower or faster, depending on a few variables. Keep in mind, though, that it will use data on your cell phone plan. If you have a limited data plan that charges you per megabyte if you go over the limit, you could run up some big charges using this method for your internet access. In other words, don't watch or download movies using your smartphone's hotspot unless you have an unlimited data plan.

Security Tips for Wi-Fi hotspots:

1. Confirm the network name with the host or merchant before you log in.
2. Make sure no one is spying on you by watching as you type in your passwords to your operating system, email, or other accounts.
3. Don't engage in financial transactions or any other sensitive transactions at a public hotspot.

Physical Security

A word about physical security while in a hotspot location and while traveling to and from the location: never leave your devices unattended! It only takes a few seconds for a crook to walk away with your goods. This applies to your car as well. Don't leave laptops or digital devices in plain view in a car, even for a short time. In many places, criminals wait in parking lots for a harried coffee drinker to run into a coffee shop and get their morning cup while leaving a laptop in plain view on the front seat. You might think a locked car is a deterrent, but this is not so, as a window can be broken in a second. Breaking windows to steal things is so common with crooks that there is a name for it: smash and grab. Don't be a victim – keep your valuables out of plain view or carry them with you.

Jeff Lanza

Chapter 12
Antivirus Software

"Oh liberty! Is it well to leave the gates unguarded?"

Thomas Bailey Aldrich

Antivirus software, which we will just call "AV," is used to prevent, detect and remove malicious software from computer systems. There are several distinct varieties of malicious software, of which viruses are just one type. Current AV software, which most of us use to protect our home computers from viruses, also protects computers against numerous other types of malicious software. I imagine it got the name "antivirus" because the first known threats against computer systems, recognized years before the internet, were viruses.

There was previous mention of some of these terms in Chapter 4, but in the context of AV, here are some definitions of the most common types of malicious software:

Virus – Malware that infects computers and replicates itself. It can disrupt programs that are already installed on a computer.

Worm – A virus that does not alter files, but resides in active memory and duplicates itself. Worms utilize networks to send copies of their original code to other computers, causing harm by consuming bandwidth, deleting files, and/or sending documents via email.

Trojan horse – Malicious computer code that is hidden in a computer program or file that may appear harmless. When the program is run, the malicious code is triggered, which results in the installation of the malware on your computer.

Keylogger – A program that is designed to capture your keystrokes as you type on a keyboard and send them to a third party. Hackers use keyloggers to steal sensitive information, such as usernames and passwords.

Rootkit - A rootkit is a type of malware designed to burrow deep into a computer, which can help it avoid being detected by AV. It may not even show up in a task manager.

Ransomware – Malware that uses a program to encrypt files on a computer. It is generally used to extort a victim into paying a ransom to the hackers. When paid, the hackers promise to provide an encryption key to decrypt the files.

Spyware – Software that is covertly installed on a computer that collects information without your knowledge or consent.

Adware – Software that is covertly installed on your computer to deliver advertisements.

Computer operating systems software should be designed to make it hard for hackers to infect our computers with malware, but it often falls short.

AV software, therefore, is designed to protect a computer user from these common threats. But the protection it offers is not perfect. Hackers are constantly changing their malware to avoid detection by AV. We can't always count on AV to keep us safe, so we need something else in addition. Can you guess what that something else is? If you said "yourself," you are correct.

Constant Vigilance

Hackers pose a persistent threat, and the very thought of encountering them can be intimidating. After many of my presentations around the country, some people remark to me that they just don't do anything online. They don't do online banking, they don't use Facebook, and many have said that they don't even use email. This is not the answer. We don't want to let hackers beat us into submission.

I believe that we should all embrace technology, use the internet, and gain all the benefits it offers. Not only should you use online banking, but you should also use mobile banking (we will discuss mobile security in another chapter).

The key is to be careful and be vigilant. Keep your eyes open to potential threats and watch out for things that don't make sense. Don't let emotional decision making put you at risk online. It is imperative that you do these things because you are the first barrier against the hackers—the first layer of security. AV software provides a second layer of protection, but it is not foolproof.

With that being said, using AV software as our second layer of security is imperative to protect against hackers. Even the most careful person will sometimes be exposed to cyber threats. Legitimate and popular websites, such as those of news organizations, can sometimes become infected with malware, which, under some conditions, spreads to our computers when we visit those sites. This is not common, but it illustrates one of the many ways our computers can become infected, even without us making any bad decisions online. So, that is where AV software comes to the rescue. It is our second layer of security.

There are many brands of AV software, including Norton, McAfee, AVG, Bitdefender, and more. There are free versions and paid versions. Sometimes internet service providers offer these products for free with your internet service. These products are the "perimeter security" for your computer. Think of them like the locks on the doors to your home. Locks do a decent job of keeping intruders out of your house, but in reality, they're not great. If a burglar really wants to get into your house, they can get around or break through common locks. The locks provide a deterrent, but if someone were to break in, your perimeter security has been breached and no longer provides protection, as the intruder is already inside. The locks can do nothing to remove the intruder.

It's the same thing with AV software, which is like perimeter security for your computer. A skillful hacker may develop a piece of malware that your AV software doesn't recognize as a threat, so it doesn't take any action to stop it. Also, a hacker can defeat the perimeter by overwhelming AV software (in essence, by breaking through a lock).

When this happens, the AV software, like the lock on your house after a breach, no longer provides security. It is unlikely that it will be able to find and remove an intruder that has circumvented it in the first place.

Because AV software is not foolproof, you might want to consider another layer of security. That layer is another type of AV software whose specific job is to scan for malware. Some effective programs for this purpose are Malwarebytes and HitmanPro. There are free versions of these programs that work alongside your AV software to eliminate threats that have circumvented the perimeter security that it provides.

Please note that the "scan only" versions of these programs are designed to scan for malware. They do not conflict or interfere with regular AV software and provide no perimeter protection. And the computer user must initiate the scan, since these programs don't actively run otherwise.

I should mention that I have no connection to the companies that make any of the products I mentioned. I do not receive any payment for referring to them in this book. I simply believe, and many security experts agree with me, that these programs are essential in providing an extra layer of security to protect your computer.

Windows Security

In recent years, Microsoft has begun providing AV software for free to people who use their operating systems.

If you are using Windows Vista or version 7 or higher, you have access to this free software. It is called Windows Defender and it is part of the Windows Essentials package.

In most cases, Defender is already on your computer, if you are using software version 8.1 or version 10. If you are using version 7, you may have to download it from Microsoft's website, but it is still provided for free.

Windows Defender is a perimeter security AV product. You cannot use it if you have other AV perimeter programs. You would have to disable any other perimeter security programs before activating Defender. You shouldn't run two perimeter antivirus programs at the same time, because they compete for computer resources and may conflict with one another.

Malwarebytes and HitmanPro (the "scan only" versions) can be used with Defender, as they can with other perimeter programs, because they only scan for malware that has gotten past perimeter defenses, so they don't conflict with the perimeter programs themselves.

Apple Computers

It is often stated that Apple computers are less vulnerable to malware. One explanation is that because there are so many more Windows-based computers in use, hackers focus on writing malware for them and less on malware for Apple products. However, this assertion does not mean that Apple computers are immune to malware, and users should consider the use of AV software in this environment.

One way that Apple helps to reduce instances of computer infection is by providing an option on the settings page which allows you to restrict downloads to those coming from the Apple Store or Apple-approved developers. This is a way to help prevent infection, as malware is commonly distributed through downloaded applications.

Updating Your Defenses

Regardless of what AV product or products you are using for your perimeter security and for scanning for intruders, it is important that these products are kept up to date. The companies that make these products are constantly monitoring what the hackers have developed to get past their defense and they adapt their products to help you stay safe against the latest threats. We employ these adaptations through the AV software update process, which should occur automatically, but may not, especially for free versions of the software.

You should check the settings of your AV software and ensure that it is set to update automatically. There should be an option for this setting. If there isn't, you must remember to update it yourself regularly. To do this, again, check the settings section of your AV software.

Speaking of updates, it is also very important to keep your operating software updated. Microsoft and Apple don't just market a computer operating system and forget about it. They tweak it, fix it and add defenses to it in the weeks and months after their marketing departments have sold it to us. If you don't keep your operating system updated, you won't have the tweaks, fixes and most importantly, the defenses against the latest hacker threats.

On the settings page in a Windows or an Apple computer there should be a drop-down menu or toggle for automatic updates. Ensure that this feature is turned on.

Chapter Summary

There are several distinct types of malware that can infect a computer and cause major problems. Your first and most important layer of security is you. Most computer infections occur when a user clicks in the wrong place. The key is to be careful, be vigilant, and watch where you click. AV software provides a second layer of security and software that finds intruders provides a third layer. For the best defense, it is important to keep your operating system and your AV programs updated to the latest versions.

Chapter 13
Mobile Security

Technology can be our best friend, and technology can also be the biggest party pooper of our lives. It interrupts our own story, interrupts our ability to have a thought or a daydream, to imagine something wonderful, because we're too busy bridging the walk from the cafeteria back to the office on the cell phone.

Steven Spielberg

On January 7, 2007, Steve Jobs, the CEO of Apple, made this announcement:

"Today, we're introducing three revolutionary products… the first one is a widescreen iPod with touch controls. The second is a revolutionary mobile phone. And the third is a breakthrough Internet communications device. So, three things: a widescreen iPod with touch controls, a revolutionary mobile phone, and a breakthrough Internet communications device. An iPod, a phone, and an Internet communicator. An iPod, a phone … are you getting it? These are not three separate devices, this is one device, and we are calling it the iPhone."

Thus, the smartphone was born. Announced in classic Apple style, the iPhone changed the world.

Jobs referred to the iPhone as three devices in one, but it is many more than that. Many more. Today, using apps, a smartphone can be many things besides a music player, internet communications device, and phone. It can be a camera, video recorder, television, airline ticket, GPS, newspaper, calculator, compass, health monitor, barcode scanner, music mixer, credit card processor, library of books, currency converter, flashlight, ride share hailer, leveler, scanner, portable gaming device, walkie-talkie, alarm clock, watch, timer, calendar, photo album, board game, thermostat, guitar tuner, light meter, accelerometer, remote control, car key, hotel room key, currency, home controller, and much more.

The smartphone is a computer, and a powerful one at that. Even the first-generation iPhones had more computing power than the computers that were aboard the Apollo spacecraft that navigated astronauts to the moon—millions of times more power.

The smartphone may make us more productive and more efficient, but, as you may notice if you observe people in public places, it is also an attention-distracting eyeball hog.

I believe that the smartphone is beyond smart. I believe it has become a smart-aleck phone. For example, if you ask Siri, the talking voice of the iPhone, a question, sometimes you get a smart-aleck answer. Here is an example:

Me: Hey Siri, what is zero divided by zero?

Siri: Imagine that you have zero cookies and you split them evenly among zero friends.

Siri: How many cookies does each person get? Siri: See, it doesn't make sense.

Siri: And cookie monster is sad that there are no cookies.

Siri: And you are sad that you have no friends.

Couldn't Siri just say that zero by zero is undefined, or that you can't have zero as a denominator in a fraction because it doesn't make sense? Instead, we get a thought experiment.

Here are a few thoughts for you about protecting your portable devices.

1. Use a passcode to protect the contents of your device. A biometric identifier is also acceptable. Think about how much personal information we keep on our portable devices: names, addresses, phone numbers, pictures, bank information, passwords to various online accounts, etc. The first reaction you are likely to have if your phone is permanently lost or stolen is,

"what did I have on there that can cause me or my family problems?" If you have the device protected with a passcode, your information is safe from anyone who has your phone.

2. Use the "find my phone" feature. This will help you locate your device (phone or tablet). If the device is turned on, you can use another device to locate it. However, if you believe your digital device has been stolen and you locate it using the "find my phone" feature, do not, I repeat, do not go to that location. Report the theft to the police and let them handle it.

3. Keep a close eye on the device when in public places, especially restaurants, bars, and coffee shops. Electronic devices are targets for theft, so don't leave them unattended, even for a moment.

4. Don't respond to unsolicited text messages or phone calls. This is especially important when the request is for personal information. Always verify who the sender is through another method or call that sender back at a number you have verified.

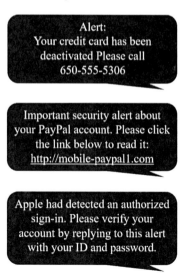

Examples of phony text messages designed to trick you into providing your personal information or login credentials to the hackers.

5. Instead of phishing, which refers to emails designed to trick you, these are referred to as "smishing," which refers to text messages designed to fool you. (Texting was originally referred to as "simple message service," or SMS. The term "smishing" comes from combining SMS with phishing.)

6. Download apps from official sites. Apple will only let you download apps from their store, which is very safe. With Android phones, you can download apps from other places besides the Google Play Store. This is not recommended, as these apps have not been vetted by Google for safety.

In 2013, theft of digital devices was at epidemic proportions, mainly in large metropolitan areas. In San Francisco, for instance, thefts of these products mostly occurred on the Muni (the local public transit system). Crooks were boldly stealing the devices right out of victims' hands on trains and buses. At the time, the police chief of San Francisco was at his wit's end. There was a media campaign to remind people to keep "Eyes Up, Phone Down." At the time, the San Francisco Police Chief, Greg Suhr, said something particularly amusing regarding the situation:

"Nobody is stealing books. If people would read a book while they're on the Muni instead of looking at their electronic device, we would get our robberies down to nothing."

Now, if you report to your cell phone provider or device manufacturer that your device has been stolen or lost, they can deactivate the device. They can turn it into a useless brick. This ability has been available for years, but it hasn't been used widely. Since its implementation, thefts of digital devices have been dramatically reduced. But digital devices are still valuable to crooks for some of their components.

Mobile Banking Security

There are different varieties of mobile banking. Let's take a look at each one and how to be secure when using them.

1. **SMS.** This is better known as texting, it allows you to communicate with your bank through text messages to do simple things like checking bank balances or receiving an alert when there is activity in your bank account. It is important to be aware that scammers will send text messages that may appear as if they are coming from a bank. They will request personal information such as a password or PIN. Never respond to these messages. When in doubt, contact your bank at a number you know to be theirs.

2. **Mobile Browser.** You can use the browser on your smartphone to do banking transactions, similar to what you might do on a computer. Most banks have optimized their websites to work in mobile format. This is generally safer than using a computer browser because smartphones are less susceptible to keystroke loggers and other risks that we see on computers. Again, it is important to always double check to make sure you are on the bank's website and not a fake. Logging in directly and not through a link will help ensure that you are on the right site.

3. **Banking apps.** If you use a banking app, you are connected directly to your bank's computers and not using a browser at all. This is considered very safe, if a few precautions are taken:

    a. Use a passcode on your mobile device
    b. Make sure your apps don't automatically log you in without a password or biometric credential.
    c. Don't save your passwords or PINs anywhere on your phone unless they are protected with a password.

d. Keep your phone's operating system updated.

e. Keep the banking apps updated.

f. Contact your bank if your phone is lost or stolen.

g. Keep in mind that banks have invested a great deal of money in making sure these apps are secure. Also, in most cases, your money is protected by bank guarantees if you report fraud with 60 days of its occurrence. Embrace the technology!

Chapter Summary

Mobile devices have made our lives more productive, more efficient, and, for the most part, more fun! But they can be time hogs and security risks. Be sure to use a passcode or biometric credential to protect the contents of your mobile device should it be lost or stolen. Don't respond to unsolicited texts or phone calls that request personal information. When using your phone for financial transactions, use the institution's mobile app if available, as it offers the most security when precautions are taken.

Summary

Cybercrime has reached epidemic proportions. The long-term effects of individual identity theft can cause a victim pain for weeks, months or longer. The key to safety, security, and being free from the hassle of victimization is prevention. I hope this book has helped you to be better at prevention. Gaining a general awareness and changing a few habits, if necessary, should help keep you safer. That was the goal of this book, to keep you safer, prevent crimes, and maybe, just maybe, take us at least a short distance down the road to putting the hackers out of business.

Ultimately, it will take more than just you and me. It must be a collaboration. Businesses need to do a better job of protecting their computers and networks. They must protect their money and keep our personal information safe. They must also do a better job of educating their employees, who tend to be a weak link, about actions to avoid online. In short, they need to make cyber security a top priority, and, more than that, they need to create a culture of security. We can't be safe unless people are thinking about security all the time. None of us should never let our guard down.

Computer manufacturers and the makers of antivirus software need to step up their game too, and help protect us with better products and more layers of security. For example, why is it possible for a hacker to remotely encrypt files on a victim's computer without the computer at least asking for its owner's permission?

Additionally, the government needs to work to put more diplomatic pressure on countries that protect hackers. It is also incumbent upon our government institutions to do more to protect their own computers and networks, as they too are often victims of breaches and fraud. Case and point – the 2014 hack into the Office of Personal Management computers, which put the personal information of 21 million people in the hands of the cyber crooks, including me.

Moreover, our federal government must take steps to limit vulnerability. Removing social security numbers from Medicare cards is a step in the right direction, but more must be done. For example, there should be restrictions on medical offices using social security numbers as patient identifiers, as their storage, in both electronic and physical formats, puts patients at risk of fraud.

For us, it comes down to a few key things, as outlined in this book. Don't let emotions overcome your logic and common sense. Don't provide personal information, money, or access to anyone who contacts you unsolicited. Watch where you click online, use up-to-date antivirus software, and keep your operating system updated on your computer and your mobile devices. Never log in through a computer link. Even better, activate two-factor authentication where possible to make your login credentials more secure. Use strong passwords and store them securely. Avoid accessing personal information on public Wi-Fi networks. Finally, protect your social security number and take action if you think it is at risk. Credit freezes are your best option in this regard.

This is a good start for preventing cybercrime and identity theft. Law enforcement can't do it alone. If we do these things as individuals, and organizations also do their part, then maybe we can start putting those hackers out of business.

Appendix A
Preventing Identity Theft

1. Protect Your Personal Information
    - Don't carry your social security card.
    - Don't provide your social security number to anyone unless there is a legitimate need for it.
2. Protect Your Documents
    - Shred your sensitive trash with a cross-cut or micro-cut shredder.
    - Don't leave outgoing mail with personal information in your mailbox for pickup.
3. Be Vigilant Against Tricks
    - Never provide personal information to anyone in response to an unsolicited request.
    - Never reply to unsolicited emails from unknown senders or open their attachments.
    - Don't click on links in emails from unknown senders.
4. Protect Your Communications
    1. Keep your computer and security software updated.
    2. Don't conduct sensitive transactions on a computer that is not under your control.
    3. Protect your Wi-Fi with a strong password and WPA2 encryption.
5. Protect Your Digital World

- Use strong passphrases with at least eight characters.
- Use different passphrases for each of your various accounts.
- If you store passphrases in a file on your computer, encrypt the file when you save it and assign a strong passphrase to protect that file.
- Consider using a passphrase management program.

Appendix B
Credit Reporting Bureaus

Credit Reporting Bureaus

Equifax: (800) 525-6285
P.O. Box 740241 Atlanta, GA 30374
Experian: (888) 397-3742
P.O. Box 9530 Allen, TX 75013
TransUnion: (800) 680-7289
P.O. Box 2000, Chester, PA 19016
Innovis: 1-800-540-2505
P.O. Box 1640 Pittsburgh, PA 15230

You are allowed one free credit for free during any 12-month period (one from each agency).

To order online: www.annualcreditreport.com To order by phone: 1-877-322-8228

Note: Innovis only provides credit reports ordered directly from them.

Terms to Understand:

Fraud Alert: Your credit file at the credit reporting agencies is flagged and a potential lender should take steps to verify that you have authorized the request. Fraud alerts only work if the merchant pays attention and takes steps to verify the identity of the applicant. They expire in 90 days unless you have been a victim of identity theft, in which case you can file an extended alert, which lasts for seven years. To place a fraud alert on your account with three credit reporting agencies, go to www.fraudalerts.equifax.com. You must contact Innovis directly to place a fraud alert at that agency.

Credit Monitoring: Your credit files are monitored by a third party and if activity occurs you are notified. There are many companies that provide this service, usually for a monthly fee, which varies widely.

Credit Freeze: A total lockdown of new account activity in your name and a proven way to protect against identity theft. Freezing prevents third parties from accessing your credit report, with some exceptions. You must unfreeze (lift) your credit report if you are engaging in activity that requires a credit check. Credit freezes are now free in all 50 states.

Appendix C
Computer Safety Tips

General Rules for Computer Security

1. Never go to a login page through a link in an email or a pop-up. Always go to the login page directly by typing the site name or, preferably, through a stored bookmark that you have created.
2. If you were not looking for it, then don't download it.
3. Keep your software current with the latest updates.
4. Don't click on links in emails from unknown senders.
5. Be cautious when clicking on links in emails from known senders, as their accounts may have been hijacked.
6. Keep your PC protected with Windows Defender or antivirus software from a third party.
7. Use CTRL+ALT+DEL to exit a pop-up safely in Windows.
8. Use CMD+OPT+ESC to exit a pop-up safely on a Mac.

Specific Actions to Avoid Online

1. Don't click on a message that seems weird. If it seems unusual for a friend to post a link, that friend may have gotten their site hijacked.
2. Don't enter your password through a link. Just because a page on the internet looks like Facebook for example, that doesn't mean it is. It is best to go the Facebook login page through your browser.
3. Don't reuse the same password on different sites. If you do this, phishers or hackers who gain access to one of your accounts may be able to access your other accounts as well, including your bank accounts. For the

highest security, you should have a different password for each of your online accounts. If you don't want to go that far, have at least ten unique passwords for distinct categories of your online life. Those categories are detailed in Chapter 9.

4. Don't click on links or open attachments in suspicious emails. Fake emails can be very convincing, and hackers can spoof the "From:" address so the email looks like it's from a social networking site. If the email looks weird, don't trust it. Delete it.

5. Don't send money anywhere unless you have verified the story of someone who says they are your friend or relative.

Common Threats

1. Fake Notification E-mails. Watch out for fake emails that look like they came from Facebook. These typically include links to phony pages that attempt to steal your login information or prompt you to download malware. Never click on links in suspicious emails. Log in to a site directly.

2. Suspicious Posts and Messages. Look out for wall posts or messages that appear to come from a friend asking you to click on a link to check out a new photo or video that doesn't actually exist. The link is typically for a phony login page or a site that will put a virus on your computer to steal your passwords.

3. Money Transfer Scams. Be suspicious of messages that appear to come from friends or others claiming to be stranded and asking for money. These messages are typically from scammers. Ask them a question that only they would be able to answer. Or, contact the

person by phone to verify the situation, even if they say not to call them.

General Online Safety Rules

1. Be wary of strangers - The internet makes it easy for people to misrepresent their identities and motives. If you interact with strangers, be cautious about the amount of information you reveal.
2. Be skeptical - People may post false or misleading information about assorted topics. Try to verify the authenticity of any information before taking any action.
3. Evaluate your settings - Use privacy settings. The default settings for some sites may allow anyone to see your profile. Private information could be exposed, so don't post anything that you wouldn't want the public to see.

Social Networking Security Reminders

1. Log in directly, not through links.
2. Only connect to people you know and trust.
3. Don't put your email address, physical address, phone number, or other personal information in your profile.
4. Sign out of your account after you use a public computer.

Ransomware

This fraud scheme begins when the victim clicks on an infected advertisement, email, or attachment, or visits an infected website. Once infected with the ransomware, the victim's files become encrypted. In most cases, once the victim pays a ransom fee, they regain access to the files that were encrypted. Here are three ways to stay protected:

1. Be wary of clicking on suspicious links or pop-ups. Sometimes these come in the form of a package delivery notification from major brand names like Amazon, FedEx, or UPS.
2. Enable pop-up blockers. Pop-ups are regularly used by criminals to spread malicious software.
3. Always back up the content on your computer. If you are infected by ransomware, you can have your system wiped clean and then restore your files from your backup. Also, because ransomware can infect all hard drives, either disconnect your backup drive when not in use or use cloud backup.

Acknowledgements

In 2018 alone, I presented the topics of identity theft and cyber security over one hundred times, mostly in places that I don't call home. The contents of this book, to a great extent, are derived from the continuing research that was necessary to present on those topics. Neither the speeches, nor this book would have been possible without support of my wife Pam and my two children, Christopher and Angela.

My father, who passed away in 2016, is a constant beacon of inspiration as he instilled in me the value of achievement through hard work. My brother Tommy, a special needs child, and one of five boys in my family, was a kind soul that is missed. He also passed away in 2016.

A shout out to Kerry Philben, the astute and skillful editor of this book and my first, "Pistols to Press".

About Jeff Lanza

Quick Bites:

- *An FBI Special Agent for over 20 years.*
- *Investigated cybercrime, fraud, organized crime, human trafficking and terrorism.*
- *Appears regularly on CNBC's Closing Bell and Power Lunch, the Fox News Channel and has appeared on Larry King Live, the Today Show and Good Morning America.*
- *Has lectured at Princeton and Harvard Universities.*
- *A published author of a critically acclaimed book.*
- *Consulted for Oscar winning movie director Ang Lee.*
- *Presented around the globe and in 49 U.S. states.*
- *Serves as a certified Kansas City barbecue judge.*

More information about Jeff:

Jeff was chosen as the best speaker in the 50-year history of Kansas City's prestigious Plaza Club. He is a professional speaker who has provided over one thousand presentations on the topics of cybercrime, identity theft, leadership ethics, crisis communication, body language and more. His clients include Ivy Investments, American Century Investments, 20th Century Fox Entertainment, UBS, Merrill Lynch, Morgan Stanley, Nationwide, Citigroup, The Young Presidents Organization, American Century, Hallmark, H & R Block, Hess Oil, Standard and Poor's, Financial Executives International, U.S. Bank, Wells Fargo and others. He developed and presented a program on identity theft prevention which was used to educate a nationwide audience of Citigroup employees. His program on the topic of leadership integrity has been certified for education credits across the United States. Jeff was the 2017 International Keynote Speaker for a cyber security road show in Australia, during which he spoke to businesses about cybercrime prevention.

Jeff was head of operations security for the Kansas City FBI and a graduate of the world-renowned John E. Reid School of Interviewing and Interrogation. He is a certified FBI instructor and has trained numerous government agencies and corporate clients on how to interpret and project body language for more effective interpersonal communication.

In addition to his latest book, Jeff authored speeches for FBI executives and has been published in The Kansas City Star, Ingram's Magazine and on the FBI National Web site.

Jeff consulted for academy award winning director Ang Lee during the production of "Ride with the Devil", and he has provided regular consulting services for television and movie production in Hollywood at Steele Films and Granfalloon Productions. Jeff was a major contributor and appeared on camera in an episode of The History Channel's, "America's Book of Secrets". He was featured in the companion documentary to the major theatrical release "Runner - Runner", which stars Ben Affleck and Justin Timberlake. Jeff has been featured in television commercials on the topic of fraud prevention.

Jeff was recruited by the FBI from Xerox Corporation, where he was a Computer Systems Analyst. He has an undergraduate degree in Criminal Justice from the University of New Haven (Connecticut) and a Master's Degree in Business Administration from the University of Texas.

Jeff Lanza